Russ Shipton's KEYBOARD & PIANO Course Book one

For Tracey, an inspiration...
"Uni-keyboard" notation by Russ Shipton
The special form of notation used in this book was devised by Russ Shipton.
It is copyright and can be used by permission only.

First Published 1992
© International Music Publications

International Music Publications, Southend Road, Woodford Green, Essex IG8 8HN, England

215-2-726

BOOK 1

This is the first book of a new and exciting keyboard course which will enable you to play songs - on piano or electronic keyboard - from the start. The unique chord and rhythm approach makes it easy to play with *two hands* almost immediately!

Simple Notation

Book 1 is suitable for absolute beginners, whether you are studying in a class or on your own. The system of *simple notation*, developed especially for this course, is easy to read and can be understood by students of any age. *No knowledge of music is necessary.*

Popular Songs

Well-known songs from a variety of music areas have been carefully chosen to illustrate techniques and to make learning enjoyable. Gentle grading plus clear design will help you progress easily and quickly. This first book of the course starts you off with some right hand chords and basic rhythms, then moves on to two-handed playing styles for ballads, and rock.

Layout

The layout of the course material is designed to make learning easier. Explanation and analysis plus the practice song are all contained within *facing pages*, so no inconvenient turning over is necessary. When you can play the featured song, chord sequences of additional songs are provided for more practice - enabling you to increase your repertoire rapidly.

MATCHING CASSETTE

An accompanying cassette is available for use with Book 1. It is produced and presented by Russ Shipton, with all the chords, rhythm patterns and songs recorded note-for-note. To make learning easier, the rhythm patterns and song accompaniments are demonstrated at two speeds: slowly, then up-to-tempo. You can check your understanding of the music and your standard of playing.

One track of the stereo recording contains *only* the keyboard part, while the second track contains the other band instruments. First you can hear and play along with the keyboard track, and then when you're ready you can enjoy playing along with the band!

I'm sure you'll enjoy my keyboard course, and if you practise a little each day you'll soon become an all-round keyboard player.

Have fun,

Russ Shipton

Contents

SONGS FEATURED IN THIS BOOK

Bachelor Boy	The Loco-motion
Da Doo Ron Ron	The Mountains Of Mourne
Edelweiss	My Bonnie
A Groovy Kind Of Love	Silent Night
I Love You Because	The Sloop John B.
In The Bleak Midwinter	Try To Remember
It Doesn't Matter Any More	The Wild Rover
The Joys Of Love	Wooden Heart

KEYBOARD INSTRUMENTS

You can use this course successfully whether you are playing an electronic keyboard or piano. Those of you playing an electronic keyboard have a choice of 'built-in' instrument sounds. For this course, use one of the piano sounds, but feel free to experiment with other possibilities. Book 4 examines the different sounds available and discusses when it is appropriate to use them. Some of the huge range of keyboard instruments are

Solo/Band Playing

This course will enable the keyboard student to:

a) play 'full' two-handed accompaniments for solo performance,

b) play the keyboard in a variety of modern music styles as part of a band arrangement.

For solo performance, one of the piano or organ sounds will normally be used; in a band context, one of a variety of sounds may be used.

The different styles and techniques given throughout the course can be simplified and adapted for band arrangements. The use of the keyboard specifically in a band context is discussed at the end of the course.

THE KEYBOARD

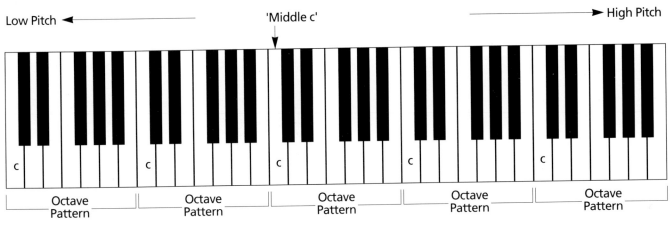

Low Pitch ◄——————► 'Middle c' ——————► High Pitch

Octave Pattern | Octave Pattern | Octave Pattern | Octave Pattern | Octave Pattern

General

The piano or synthesiser keyboard includes both black and white keys. The smaller synthesiser may have as few as 25 keys, while larger pianos have as many as 88 keys. Whatever size keyboard you are using, you'll notice that the black and white keys are organised into a repeating pattern.

Pitch

The pitch of the notes goes higher when you play the keys further to the right of the keyboard, and lower to the left. As already mentioned, the keyboard can be divided up into sections. Each section includes a set of two black keys followed by a set of three black keys, as shown above. These sections have been called 'octave patterns' because the music system organises notes into 'octaves'. All notes an octave apart in pitch are given the same name because they sound so similar to each other - even though they are some distance in pitch apart. Try playing the **c** notes shown above and see how similar they sound.

PLAYING POSITION

You should feel comfortable when playing. Sit up high enough to reach the keys easily. Keep your back straight and have your feet flat on the floor. Find a stool or chair that's the right height for you, or if you have an adjustable synthesiser stand, change the height of the keyboard to suit you.

In this book you'll be playing around '**middle c**' (indicated above), so position yourself opposite the middle of the keyboard.

THE NAMES OF NOTES

The first seven letters of the alphabet (**a** to **g**) are used to name notes. They are given to the notes produced by the white keys on the keyboard:

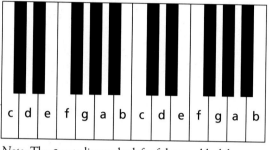

Note: The **c** note lies to the left of the two black keys.

Repeating Octaves

Each 'repeating octave pattern' consists of the same seven notes in the same relative position. As a first and easy step in remembering the keyboard notes, remember that the **c** note always lies just to the left of the set of two black keys. Later, as you play the chords and bass notes in this book, you'll gradually start to remember where all the other notes are in relation to **c** without counting along.

Black Key Notes

The black keys have sharp or flat names. The material in much of this book involves just the white keys, so for the moment you don't have to worry about sharps or flats.

FINGER INDICATIONS *(Right Hand)*

The standard finger indications are used in this course. For the moment you'll need to know the numbers given to each finger on your right hand:

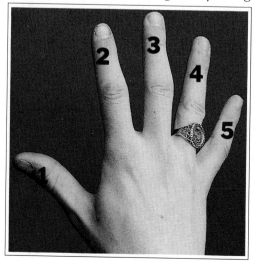

Hand Position

Hold your right hand out and try pressing down some keys with your fingertips. Keep the back of your hand and forearm horizontal, and arch your fingers. Hold them in a curved shape as if you're holding a ball. Pressing down with the thumb involves using some of the side of the thumb as well as the pad.

Long nails can prevent the fingertips pressing down on the keys properly, so you should *keep your fingernails short*.

Basic Chords & Rhythms

CHORDS *(for the Right Hand)*

Chords are essential for modern music. They are used as a basis for composing songs as well as for rhythmic and harmonic accompaniment of the melody line. A chord is produced when three or more notes are played at the same time.

To begin with we're going to look at chords for the right hand. Right hand chords are used by all modern players - whether playing solo or in a band, and whether playing a piano or elctronic keyboard.

The most common and 'ordinary' sounding chords are called 'major' chords. Try your first chord, the **C** major chord (**C** for short):

The C (Major) Chord

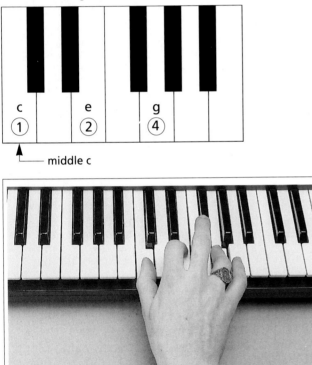

middle c

Place your right hand thumb ① on the **c** note key (**middle c**), your index finger ② on the **e** note, and your ring finger ④ on the **g** note as shown. Press all three keys down at *exactly* the same time, and then release them all at the same time.

Try playing the **C** chord several times. When you play the chord, remember to keep your fingers arched and the back of your hand and forearm horizontal. The fingers you aren't using should be kept reasonably straight and a little above the keyboard.

Here is a wider view of the **C** chord position on the keyboard:

3-BEAT RHYTHM

Song accompaniments usually involve one of two important rhythms. Perhaps the simpler of the two is the 3-beat rhythm - the regular beats of the accompaniment are divided into groups of three, with the 1st beat of each group being stressed more than the other two i.e. 1 2 3 1 2 3 1 2 3 etc. This is the rhythm used for a waltz.

Using simple notation, here's how a basic 3-beat rhythm pattern looks:

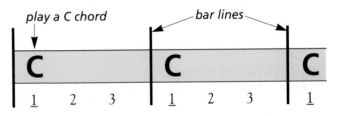

The large '**C**' represents the whole **C** chord. Play the **C** chord and count '1' on the 1st beat of each group of three. Tap your foot on each beat and count '2' & '3' on the other two beats as shown. For the moment you can hold the chord down for three beats, till just before the following 1st beat. *

Each group of three beats makes up what is called a 'bar' - the lines dividing up the groups are known as bar lines. *Make sure you keep the beats regular and evenly spaced* - take the tempo at about walking pace i.e. not too fast.

*Note: Electronic keyboard players should use a piano sound to start with. See the note on page 4.

THREE MAIN CHORDS

Many songs can be played with only three chords. When the **C** chord that you've just learnt is the 'key' chord i.e. where the accompaniment ends on a **C** chord and the melody ends on a **c** note, the other two main chords are **F** (major) and **G** (major). You can use exactly the same fingering for these chords as you did for the **C** chord, just move your hand to the right:

The F (Major) Chord

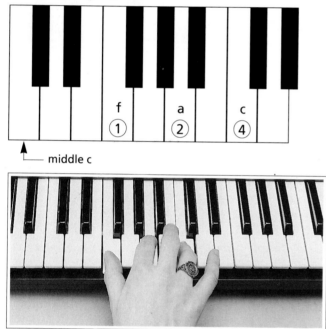

⌐— middle c

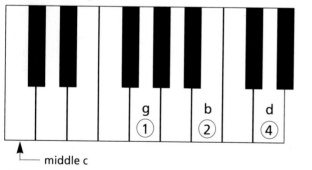

The G (Major) Chord

middle c

For the **F** chord, place your thumb ① on the **f** note above **middle c** and your index ② on the **a** note. The **c** note is pressed down by your ring finger ④. You'll see that the fingering is the same as for the **C** chord.

The fingering is the same for the **G** chord as for the **C** and **F** chords - place your thumb ① on the **g** note above **middle c**, your index ② on the **b** and your ring finger ④ on the **d** note.

Changing Chords

Try to commit the **C**, **F** & **G** chords to memory, and then have a go at changing from one to another. Keep your fingers the same distance apart while your hand moves - make sure your thumb goes to the right key, and then the other fingers will automatically land on the correct keys too!

When you're happy with the chord changes, you're ready for your first song accompaniment - "The Joys Of Love". This involves the 3-beat rhythm pattern that you played on page 7, and just the **C**, **F** & **G** chords.

The Joys Of Love

Count the rhythm as shown and play each chord on the 1st beat of the bar. Tap your foot on each beat and hold the chord down for the whole bar, releasing it and moving as quickly as you can to the next chord position in time for the 1st beat of the bar again.

Once you're doing the chord changes reasonably smoothly and keeping the rhythm going slowly but steadily, then you can try humming the tune or singing the words at the same time as playing the accompaniment. Here are the melody notes: *

The joys of love last just a moment or two
g c d e f f f e c e d
The pain of love will last your whole life through.
g a b c d e a d f   e d   c

*Note: The songs in this course have been chosen because they are both popular and melodic, but should you need help in following the melody and accompaniments, there is a cassette available for use with each book.

Basic Chords & Rhythms

THE JOYS OF LOVE
Traditional, arranged by Russ Shipton

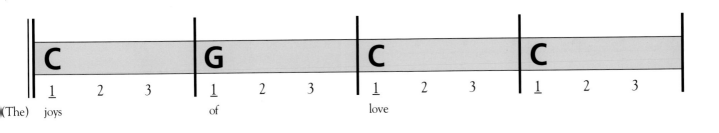

C	G	C	C
1 2 3	1 2 3	1 2 3	1 2 3
(The) joys	of	love	

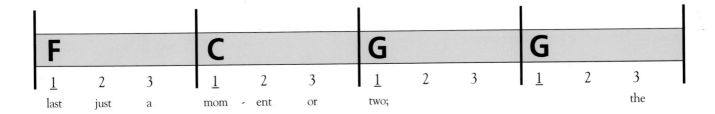

F	C	G	G
1 2 3	1 2 3	1 2 3	1 2 3
last just a	mom - ent or	two;	the

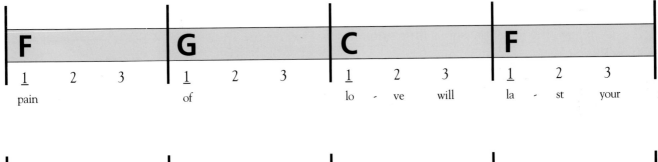

F	G	C	F
1 2 3	1 2 3	1 2 3	1 2 3
pain	of	lo - ve will	la - st your

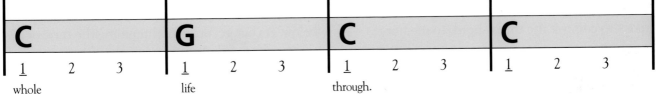

C	G	C	C
1 2 3	1 2 3	1 2 3	1 2 3
whole	life	through.	

Note: Sing 'The' first, then play the **C** chord as you sing 'joys'. When you can sing and play the 1st verse, turn to the back of the book for the other verses.

ADDITIONAL SONGS

Many accompaniments can be played in a 3-beat rhythm with just the **C, F & G** chords. When you've mastered "The Joys Of Love", try playing these songs in a similar way. The chord sequences for some of them are given in the back of the book.

MULL OF KINTYRE (Paul McCartney)
AMAZING GRACE (Judy Collins)
SO LONG, IT'S BEEN GOOD TO KNOW YOU (Traditional)
HOME ON THE RANGE (Traditional)
HAPPY BIRTHDAY TO YOU (M. & P Hill).

3-BEAT RHYTHM PATTERN

Another way of playing the 3-beat rhythm is to sound a chord on every beat of the bar, like this:

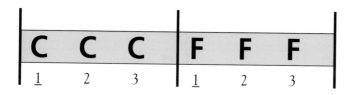

C	C	C	F	F	F
1	2	3	1	2	3

Count the rhythm '1 2 3' as before, but this time press the keys down on every beat count - as you tap your foot. Keep the tempo steady and the beats evenly spaced. Hold the keys down and only release them *just* before the following beat.

1st Beat Stress

If you're playing a piano or 'touch sensitive' electronic keyboard, press the keys down harder for more volume on the 1st beat of each bar. Those of you with an ordinary keyboard can get a similar stress effect by shortening the notes on the 2nd and 3rd beats - release the finger pressure a little earlier than on the 1st beat:

Beat	1	2	3
	long	short	short

Chord Reminder

Here's a reminder of the C, F & G chord positions. But try to commit the three chords to memory...

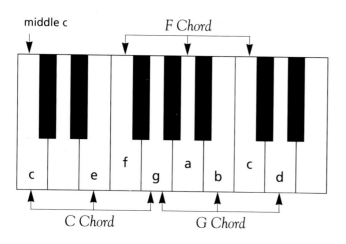

CLIFF RICHARD

Bachelor Boy

The melody of each verse of "Bachelor Boy" varies slightly. The notes of the first two verses are given below. As before, don't try humming the tune or singing the words until you can play the sequence steadily and smoothly.

When I was young my father said
  c c c e f g gaad

"Son, I have something to say"
  b b a g g f e

And what he told me I'll never forget
  c c c e f g ag f a

Until my dying day.
  a g g d e d c

He said: "Son, you are a bachelor boy
ga b c e f g a g f a

And that's the way to stay
  a a b a g f e a g

Son, you be a bachelor boy
  c e f g a g f a

Until your dying day."
  a g f d e d c

10

Simple Chord Style

BACHELOR BOY

Words and Music by Bruce Welch and Cliff Richard

C	C	C	C	C	C	F	F	F	F	F	F
1	2	3	1	2	3	1	2	3	1	2	3

When I was you - ng my fath - er said,
"Son, you are a bach - e - lor boy, and

G	G	G	G	G	G	C	C	C	C	C	C
1	2	3	1	2	3	1	2	3	1	2	3

"Son, I have some - thing to say."
that's the way to stay.

C	C	C	C	C	C	F	F	F	F	F	F
1	2	3	1	2	3	1	2	3	1	2	3

And what he told me I'll nev - er for - get un -
Son, you be a bach - e - lor boy, un -

G	G	G	G	G	G	C	C	C	G	G	G
1	2	3	1	2	3	1	2	3	1	2	3

til my dy - ing day. He said:
til your dy - ing day.

Note: When you can sing and play the sequence for "Bachelor Boy", turn to the back of the book for the other lyrics of the song.

ADDITIONAL SONGS

As well as those given on page 9, here is a list of other well-known songs you can play in the same way as "Bachelor Boy". The chord sequences for some of these songs are given in the back of the book.

THERE GOES MY EVERYTHING (Elvis Presley)
LAVENDER BLUE (Traditional)
CLEMENTINE (Traditional)
AWAY IN A MANGER (Traditional)
I'M SO LONESOME I COULD CRY (Hank Williams).

11

THE 4-BEAT RHYTHM

Most song accompaniments involve the 4-beat rhythm. Here the regular beats are divided into groups or bars of four, with the 1st beat in each bar stressed a little more than the other three i.e. 1 2 3 4, 1 2 3 4, 1 2 3 4, etc.

Using the same simple notation with the same **C**, **F** & **G** chords that you know, this is how a basic 4-beat rhythm pattern looks:

C				F				G
1	2	3	4	1	2	3	4	1

THE BEACH BOYS

Play the usual **C** chord with your right hand and count '1'. Tap your foot on each beat as before and count '2 3 4' on the other beats as indicated.

Hold each chord down for the whole bar i.e. four beats, and then quickly change to the next chord on the 1st beat of the following bar. As with the 3-beat rhythm, make sure you *keep the beats regular and evenly spaced*. Don't go too fast.

Changing Chords

As before, keep your thumb and fingers in the same relative position as you move along the keyboard to the different major chords. Aim for the root note of each chord (where the thumb goes), and the other fingers should automatically fall on the right keys.

Melody Level

You may be finding the melody notes in the key of **C** major a little high (or low) for your vocal range. Towards the end of the book another key is introduced and you'll be able to change the accompaniments you've been struggling to sing with to the new and more comfortable key!

The Sloop John B.

This Beach Boys classic has a chorus with more or less the same melody as the verse:

We come on the Sloop John B.
g   e e   e   f e

My grandpappy and me
g   e   e   e f e

Round Nassau Town we did roam
e   e f   g   g f e   d

Drinking all night, got into a fight
g   a b   c   c d e f

Oh I feel so broke up, I wanna go home.
f f e e   e   c d d c b   c

Simple Chord Style

THE SLOOP JOHN B.
Traditional, arranged by Russ Shipton

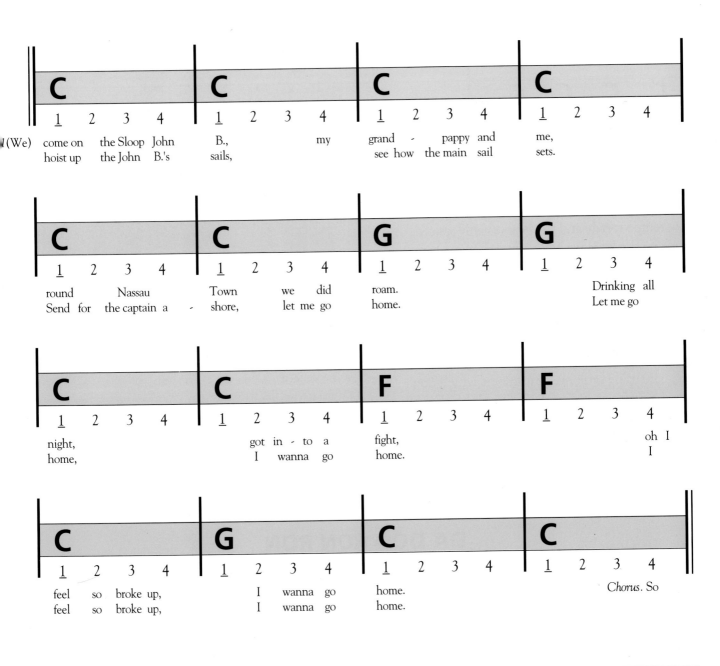

C	C	C	C
1 2 3 4	1 2 3 4	1 2 3 4	1 2 3 4

(We) come on the Sloop John B., my grand - pappy and me,
hoist up the John B.'s sails, see how the main sail sets.

C	C	G	G
1 2 3 4	1 2 3 4	1 2 3 4	1 2 3 4

round Nassau Town we did roam. Drinking all
Send for the captain a - shore, let me go home. Let me go

C	C	F	F
1 2 3 4	1 2 3 4	1 2 3 4	1 2 3 4

night, got in - to a fight, oh I
home, I wanna go home. I

C	G	C	C
1 2 3 4	1 2 3 4	1 2 3 4	1 2 3 4

feel so broke up, I wanna go home. *Chorus.* So
feel so broke up, I wanna go home.

ADDITIONAL SONGS

Many popular songs can be played with just the **C, F** & **G** chords in a 4-beat rhythm. When you've been through the chord sequence for "The Sloop John B.", try playing these songs in a similar way - the chord sequences for some of them are given in the back of the book, together with the other verses of "The Sloop John B."

LEAVING ON A JET PLANE (John Denver)
TOM DOOLEY (The Kingston Trio)
HUSH LITTLE BABY (Traditional)
THE LAST THING ON MY MIND (Tom Paxton)
ROCK AROUND THE CLOCK (Bill Haley)
A LITTLE PEACE (Nicole).

4-BEAT RHYTHM PATTERN

As you did with the 3-beat rhythm, another way of playing the 4-beat rhythm is to sound a chord on every beat of the bar, like this:

C	C	C	C
<u>1</u>	2	3	4

Count the pattern '1 2 3 4' as before, but this time press down the chord keys on all the beats - at the same time as you tap your foot. As usual, try to keep the tempo steady and the beats evenly spaced. Release the keys *just* before the following beat.

1st Beat Stress

To produce the 'natural' stress for the 4-beat rhythm, you need to press down harder on the 1st beat of each bar. This variation of stress also helps to make the accompaniment more interesting. Those of you who are using ordinary synthesisers which don't have 'touch sensitivity' should hold the chord on the 1st beat of each bar for the full length, and cut the other three short by releasing the keys early:

Beat	<u>1</u>	*2*	*3*	*4*
	long	short	short	short

THE CRYSTALS

Da Doo Ron Ron

When you can play the chord sequence for "Da Doo Ron Ron" steadily and evenly, have a go at singing the words or humming the tune at the same time.

I met him on a Monday and my heart stood still
e e e e e e d c d c c

Da doo ron ron ron, da doo ron ron
c d d d e d c c

Somebody told me that his name was Bill *(Repeat 2nd line)*
e e e e d c d c c

Yeah, my heart stood still, yeah, his name was Bill
e c d c c e c e d d

And when he walked me home *(Repeat 2nd line)*.
e d e d c c

DA DOO RON RON
Words and Music by Phil Spector, Jeff Barry, Ellie Greenwich

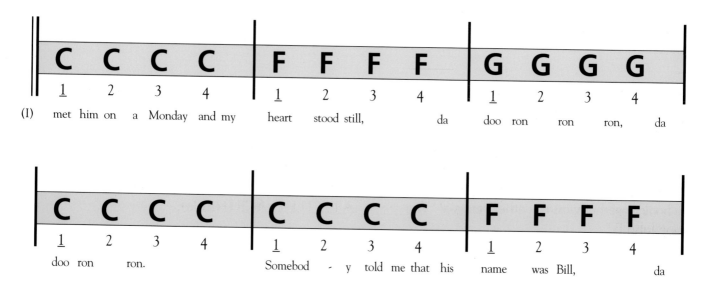

C	C	C	C	F	F	F	F	G	G	G	G
<u>1</u>	2	3	4	<u>1</u>	2	3	4	<u>1</u>	2	3	4

(I) met him on a Monday and my | heart stood still, da | doo ron ron ron, da

C	C	C	C	C	C	C	C	F	F	F	F
<u>1</u>	2	3	4	<u>1</u>	2	3	4	<u>1</u>	2	3	4

doo ron ron. | Somebod - y told me that his | name was Bill, da

DA DOO RON RON
(Continued)

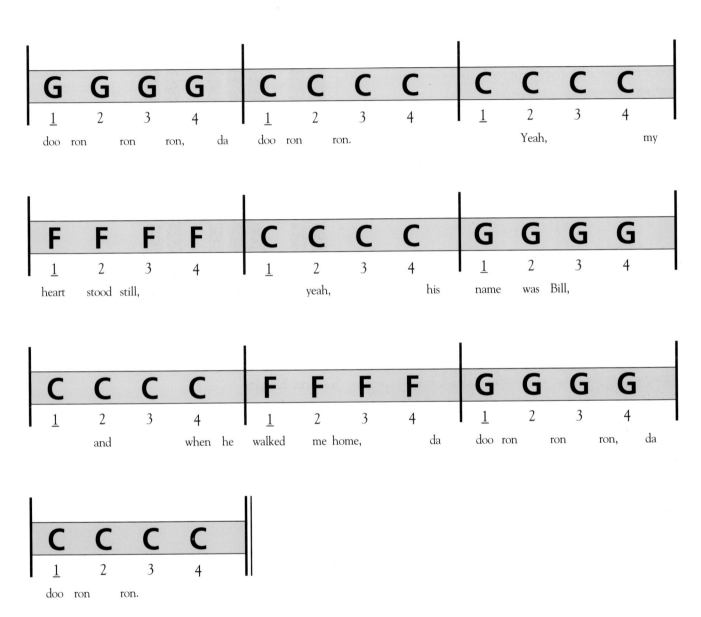

Note: When changing chords you must make sure you're keeping a steady rhythm with evenly spaced beats - *don't* go fast only to stop before each chord change!

ADDITIONAL SONGS

As well as those given on page 13, here is a list of other well-known songs you can play in the same way as "Da Doo Ron Ron". The chord sequences for some of these songs are given in the back of the book together with the other verses of "Da Doo Ron Ron".

GREEN GREEN GRASS OF HOME (Tom Jones)
BLOWIN' IN THE WIND (Bob Dylan)
HEARTBREAK HOTEL (Elvis Presley)
THE RIDDLE SONG (Traditional)
AULD LANG SYNE (Traditional).

MINOR CHORDS

The simple 3-note major chords that you've been using are in a sense the most 'normal' sounding of the various types of chord that can be played. The other group of extremely common chords are 'minor' chords. These sound slightly 'sad' compared to the major chords. Play the **D** minor (**Dm**) chord and listen to the sound:

The D Minor Chord (Dm)

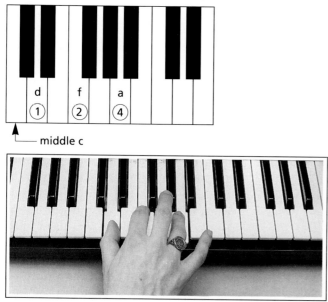

— middle c

Notice that you can use the same fingering for **D** minor (and the other two minor chords) as you did for the major chords.

As well as the *three* major chords (**C**, **F** & **G**) you will often come across *three* minor chords in the key of **C** major: **Dm**, **Em** and **Am**.

The E Minor Chord (Em)

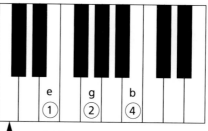

— middle c

The A Minor Chord (Am)

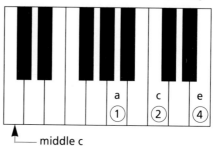

— middle c

Silent Night

Silent night, holy night, all is calm, all is bright
g a g e   g a g e   d d b   c c g
Round yon virgin mother and child (*Same melody for line 3*)
a   a c b a   g a g   e
Sleep in heavenly peace, sleep in heavenly peace.
d d f   d b   c e   c g e   g   f d   c

SILENT NIGHT
Words and Music by J. Mohr & F. Gruber, arranged by Russ Shipton

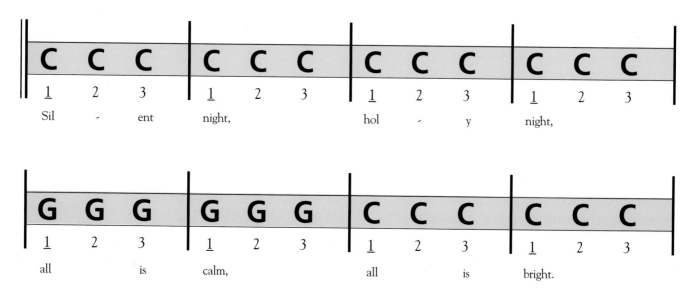

C	C	C	C	C	C	C	C	C	C	C	C
1	2	3	1	2	3	1	2	3	1	2	3
Sil	-	ent	night,			hol	-	y	night,		

G	G	G	G	G	G	C	C	C	C	C	C
1	2	3	1	2	3	1	2	3	1	2	3
all		is	calm,			all		is	bright.		

SILENT NIGHT
(Continued)

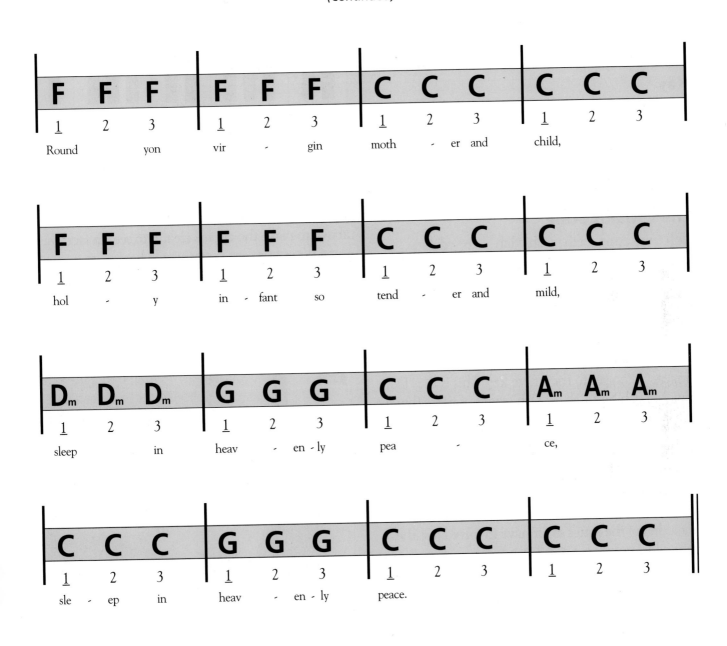

F	F	F	F	F	F	C	C	C	C	C	C
1	2	3	1	2	3	1	2	3	1	2	3
Round		yon	vir	-	gin	moth	-	er and	child,		

F	F	F	F	F	F	C	C	C	C	C	C
1	2	3	1	2	3	1	2	3	1	2	3
hol	-	y	in	-	fant	so	tend	-	er and	mild,	

D$_m$	D$_m$	D$_m$	G	G	G	C	C	C	A$_m$	A$_m$	A$_m$
1	2	3	1	2	3	1	2	3	1	2	3
sleep		in	heav	-	en - ly	pea	-		ce,		

C	C	C	G	G	G	C	C	C	C	C	C
1	2	3	1	2	3	1	2	3	1	2	3
sle	-	ep	in	heav	-	en - ly	peace.				

ADDITIONAL SONGS

A large number of popular songs - traditional and modern - can be played with major and minor chords in a 3-beat waltz rhythm. When you can play "Silent Night" steadily and smoothly, try playing the songs listed here. The chord sequences for some of them are given at the back of the book with the other verses of "Silent Night".

THE LAST WALTZ (Engelbert Humperdink)
IN DUBLIN'S FAIR CITY (Traditional)
OH DEAR, WHAT CAN THE MATTER BE? (Traditional)
THE NIGHTINGALE (Traditional)
IT'S FOUR IN THE MORNING (Faron Young).

Simple Chord Style

KEY, MELODY AND CHORDS

Before you move on and try more complicated patterns involving both left and right hands, it would be a good idea for you to understand the connection between key, chords and melody.

Key

When a tune ends on a **c** note and the last chord is a **C** (major) chord, the music is said to be 'in the key of **C** major'. This means the notes expected to be used in the melody *and* in the accompanying chords will be from the **C** major scale.

The C Major Scale

doh	ray	me	fah	soh	lah	te	doh
c	d	e	f	g	a	b	c
①	②	③	①	②	③	④	⑤

Play the notes (on the white keys) from **middle c** to the next **c** above, using the fingering given - pass your thumb ① under the index ② and middle fingers ③ to get to the **f** note key. This is the "Doh Ray Me Fah Soh Lah Te Doh" series of notes that we all learn when young.

Melody Notes

When the melody is written in the key of **C**, the expected or 'in key' notes are all white keys on the keyboard - you will have noticed that all the melodies of the songs so far have involved just the white key notes i.e. **c d e f g a b**.

Chord Notes

Not only will the melody notes come from the **C** major scale, but also the notes that make up both the major and minor chords used to accompany the melody:

Major Chords
⎧ C = c e g
⎨ F = f a c
⎩ G = g b d

Minor Chords
⎧ Dm = d f a
⎨ Em = e g b
⎩ Am = a c e

The chords in the key of **C** major are summarised on the diagram.

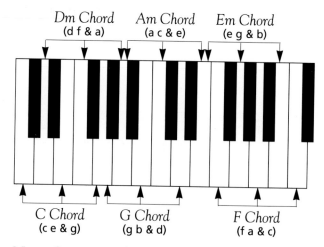

Dm Chord (d f & a) *Am Chord* (a c & e) *Em Chord* (e g & b)

C Chord (c e & g) *G Chord* (g b & d) *F Chord* (f a & c)

Notes from more than one octave have been used above to make the chords clearer to see. In fact, the same notes from *any* octave could be used in a melody or to form chords, as you'll see later.

PHIL COLLINS

A Groovy Kind Of Love

This song involves a 4-beat rhythm with major and minor chords from **C** major. All the melody notes are in key too, taken from the **C** major scale.

When I'm feeling blue, all I have to do
c d e f g f e d c b

Is take a look at you, then I'm not so blue
b c b a b c d c b c d

When you're close to me, I can hear your heart beat
d e f g a g f e d g g

I can hear you breathing in my ear
f e d c g g f e d

Wouldn't you agree, baby you and me
c d e f g f e d c b

Got a groovy kind of love, we've got a groovy kind of love.
b b c b a b c c c c c b a b c

Bass-Chord Style

A GROOVY KIND OF LOVE

Words & Music by Toni Wine & Carole Bayer-Sager

G	G	G	G		C	C	C	C		G	G	G	G
1	2	3	4		1	2	3	4		1	2	3	4

When I'm feeling blue, all I have to do is take a look at

C	C	C	C		G	G	G	G		Dm	Dm	Dm	Dm
1	2	3	4		1	2	3	4		1	2	3	4

you, then I'm not so blue. When you're close to me I can feel your

Em	Em	Em	Em		Dm	Dm	F	F		G	G	G	G
1	2	3	4		1	2	3	4		1	2	3	4

heart beat, I can hear you breath - ing in my ear. Wouldn't you a-

C	C	C	C		G	G	G	G		C	C	C	C
1	2	3	4		1	2	3	4		1	2	3	4

gree, bab - y you and me got a groovy kind of love.

(to bar 2)

G	G	G	G		C	C	C	C		G	G	G	G
1	2	3	4		1	2	3	4		1	2	3	4

We've got a groovy kind of love. *Verse 2.* An - y time you

Note: There is a change of chord in the middle of the 8th bar - play the **Dm** chord on beats 1 & 2 and the **F** chord on beats 3 & 4.

ADDITIONAL SONGS

Many great songs can be played with major and minor chords in a 4-beat rhythm. When you can play "A Groovy Kind Of Love", try some of these songs - as before, the chord sequences for some of them are given in the back of the book.

HEY JUDE (The Beatles)
LET IT BE (The Beatles)
THE WATER IS WIDE (Traditional)
THE ROSE (Bette Midler)
THE LEAVING OF LIVERPOOL (Traditional)
WHERE HAVE ALL THE FLOWERS GONE? (Pete Seeger).

USING THE LEFT HAND

A keyboard player in a band may sometimes use only his right hand. When playing on your own you need to use both hands for a full accompaniment. The left hand fingering indications are similar to those for the right hand:

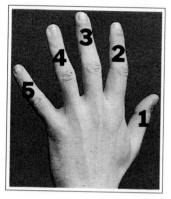

Left Hand Root Notes

To keep things simple, your left hand can play just the bass notes that match the name of the right hand chord (root notes). For a song like "The Wild Rover" for example, which involves the C, F & G chords, your left hand will play just the c, f & g notes below **middle c**:

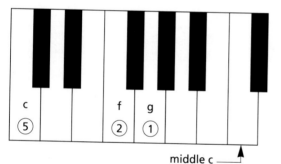

Your left hand fingers can be held over the keys in the way shown above. This means the little finger ⑤ is used for the **c** note, the index finger ② for the **f** note, and the thumb ① for the **g** note.

3-BEAT RHYTHM PATTERN

In the simple notation that we're using, each left hand bass note is shown by a small letter - as distinct from the large capital letter which indicates a right hand chord. Try this 3-beat example:

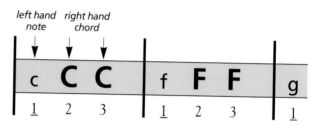

Hold your left hand fingers over the keys below **middle c** in the way shown and press the low **c** note down with your little finger ⑤. Then play the **C** chord twice (with your right hand) on the 2nd & 3rd beats of the first bar.

Count the 3-beat rhythm '1 2 3', keeping the beats steady and evenly spaced as usual. Here is the position of the two hands playing the **C** bar together:

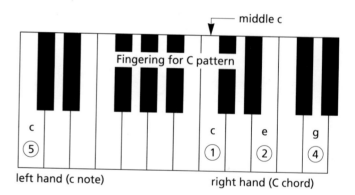

Start the **F** bars by pressing down the low **f** note with your left hand index finger ② on the 1st beat, then play two right hand chords on beats 2 & 3. The **G** bars are started with a **g** note, played by your left hand thumb ①.

The Wild Rover

I've been a wild rover for many a year
c c d c a g e e d e f

And I've spent all my money on whiskey and beer
e f g e g f d b g e d c

Chorus

And it's no, nay, never, no nay never no more
b c d d b g e e e d e f

Will I play the wild rover, no never no more.
e f g c c b a g g e d c

Bass-Chord Style

THE WILD ROVER

Traditional, arranged by Russ Shipton

Verse

c C C	c C C	c C C	f F F	f F F
1 2 3	1 2 3	1 2 3	1 2 3	1 2 3
(I've) been a wild	rov - er for	man - y a	year,	and I've
now I'm ret -	urn - ing with	gold in great	store,	and I

(Repeat 9 bars)   **Chorus**

c C C	g G G	g G G	c C C	g G G
1 2 3	1 2 3	1 2 3	1 2 3	1 2 3
spent all my	money on	whisk - ey and	beer. But /	no,
nev - er will	play the wild	rov - er no	more. And it's	

g G G	g G G	g G G	c C C	c C C
1 2 3	1 2 3	1 2 3	1 2 3	1 2 3
nay,	never,		no nay	nev - er no

f F F	f F F	c C C	c C C	f F F
1 2 3	1 2 3	1 2 3	1 2 3	1 2 3
more,	will I	play	the wild	rov - er,

f F F	c C C	g G G	c C C	c C C
1 2 3	1 2 3	1 2 3	1 2 3	1 2 3
no	never,		no	more!

ADDITIONAL SONGS

Once you've mastered "The Wild Rover", try using the simple bass-chord style for some of the 3-beat songs that were given on pages 9 & 11.

Bass-Chord Style

4-BEAT RHYTHM PATTERN

One of the many possible bass-chord patterns for 4-beat song accompaniments is a simple one that suits faster songs. In standard music notation you might see this sign at the start of the music: ₵. We're going to use this kind of pattern for the next song, "Wooden Heart":

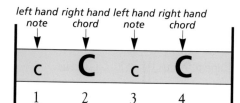

left hand note | right hand chord | left hand note | right hand chord

c	C	c	C
<u>1</u>	2	3	4

Your left hand fingers should be positioned as they were for the 3-beat bass-chord pattern that you used for the last song. The little finger ⑤ plays the low **c** note on the 1st beat, then the right hand plays the **C** chord on the 2nd beat. The low root note and chord are repeated for the other two beats.

The **F** & **G** bars are played in a similar way - try to use the correct left hand fingers for the two **f** & **g** notes.

Note Length

You can hold the left hand notes for just one beat, or you can let them ring on under the following chord. Experiment!

ELVIS PRESLEY

Wooden Heart

Can't you see I love you? Please don't break my heart in two
   c d e e g f   f a   g a g f e

That's not hard to do 'cause I don't have a wooden heart.
   g a g f e e g f   f e d g e

                  (Verse 2: e c)

Middle Section

There's no strings upon this love of mine
   c e d e f d e f g

It was always you from the start.
g g a a c b a g

WOODEN HEART

Words and Music by Fred Wise, Ben Weisman, Kay Twomey and Berthold Kaempfert

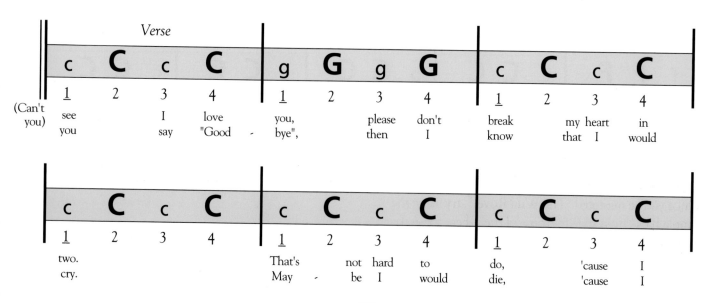

Bass-Chord Style

WOODEN HEART
(Continued)

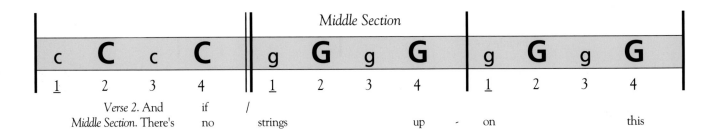

g	**G**	g	**G**		g	**G**	g	**G**		c	**C**	c	**C**
_1_	2	3	4		_1_	2	3	4		_1_	2	3	4

don't   have a   wood - en   heart.
don't   have a   wood - en   heart.

Middle Section

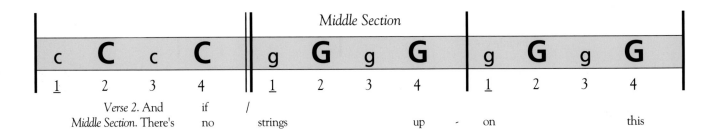

c	**C**	c	**C**		g	**G**	g	**G**		g	**G**	g	**G**
_1_	2	3	4		_1_	2	3	4		_1_	2	3	4

Verse 2. And if /
Middle Section. There's no strings   up - on   this

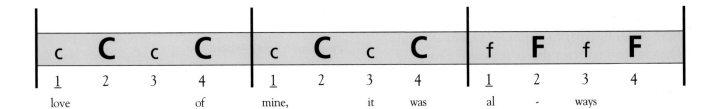

c	**C**	c	**C**		c	**C**	c	**C**		f	**F**	f	**F**
_1_	2	3	4		_1_	2	3	4		_1_	2	3	4

love   of   mine, it was   al - ways

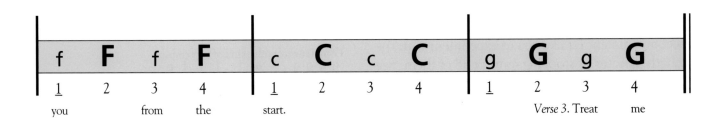

f	**F**	f	**F**		c	**C**	c	**C**		g	**G**	g	**G**
_1_	2	3	4		_1_	2	3	4		_1_	2	3	4

you   from the   start.   *Verse 3.* Treat me

ADDITIONAL SONGS

Many faster country-flavoured songs suit the simple bass-chord pattern used for "Wooden Heart". Try playing some of the well-known songs listed here. The chord sequences for some of them are given at the back of the book, and involve just the **C, F & G** chords.

I WALK THE LINE (Johnny Cash)
YOU'RE MY BEST FRIEND (Don Williams)
DON'T PASS ME BY (Ringo Starr)
JAMBALAYA ON THE BAYOU (Hank Williams)
MY OLD MAN'S A DUSTMAN
(Lonnie Donegan)
TRAVELIN' LIGHT (Cliff Richard)
THIS TRAIN (Traditional).

MINOR CHORD ROOT NOTES

Your next song involves the bass chord style with both major *and* minor chords. For the **Dm, Em** & **Am** chord, your left hand should play the **d, e** & **a** notes respectively:

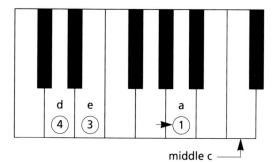

Hold your fingers in the same position as before (page 20), and use your ring finger ④ for the **d** note and middle finger ③ for the **e** note. For the **a** note, move your thumb ① up one key as shown.

Note length

Notes can be shortened or 'stopped' to produce a more dynamic rhythm or just for variety of sound. The classical term for this is 'staccato'. Stopping notes is a technique used frequently in rock music and boogies - as you'll see later in the course.

On pages 10 & 14, those of you on keyboards without 'touch sensitivity' created a stress pattern by holding the first chord of each bar and shortening the other chords. In this and the next accompaniment I'd like you to experiment with the length of notes by stopping some or all of them. See what sounds better to you and what you don't like.

To give you some ideas to start with, try these three different approaches on "Try To Remember".

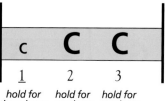

c	C	C
<u>1</u>	2	3
hold for three beats (one bar)	*hold for one beat*	*hold for one beat*

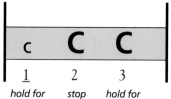

c	C	C
<u>1</u>	2	3
hold for three beats (one bar)	*stop short*	*hold for one beat*

c	C	C
<u>1</u>	2	3
hold for three beats (one bar)	*stop short*	*stop short*

Try To Remember

Try to remember the kind of September
e e e e   d c f   f f g

When life was slow and oh so mellow
a   g   e c g   g a f   d a

(Lines 3 & 4 have the same melody as 1 & 2)

Try to remember the kind of September
g g g g   f e f   f f e

When you were a tender and callow fellow
d   e   e e e d   c d d b g

Try to remember and if you remember, then follow.
e e e e   d c f   f f g a e c

TRY TO REMEMBER
Words by Tom Jones, Music by Harvey Schmidt

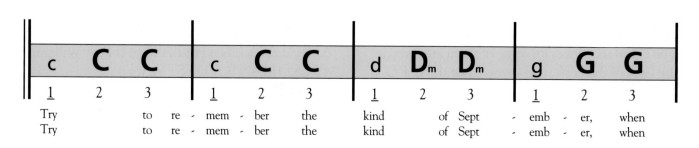

TRY TO REMEMBER

(Continued)

(Repeat 8 bars)

c	**C**	**C**	c	**C**	**C**	d	**D**m	**D**m	g	**G**	**G**
1	2	3	1	2	3	1	2	3	1	2	3

life ... was ... slow ... and ... oh ... so ... mellow.
grass ... was ... green ... and ... grain ... was ... yellow.

e	**E**m	**E**m	a	**A**m	**A**m	d	**D**m	**D**m	g	**G**	**G**
1	2	3	1	2	3	1	2	3	1	2	3

Try ... to re - memb - er ... the ... kind ... of Sept - ember, ... when

c	**C**	**C**	f	**F**	**F**	d	**D**m	**D**m	g	**G**	**G**
1	2	3	1	2	3	1	2	3	1	2	3

you ... were a tend - er ... and ... call - ow ... fellow.

c	**C**	**C**	c	**C**	**C**	d	**D**m	**D**m	g	**G**	**G**
1	2	3	1	2	3	1	2	3	1	2	3

Try ... to re - memb - er ... and ... if ... you re - memb - er, ... then

c	**C**	**C**	c	**C**	**C**	d	**D**m	**D**m	g	**G**	**G**
1	2	3	1	2	3	1	2	3	1	2	3

follow.

ADDITIONAL SONGS

When you've played through the chord sequence for "Try To Remember", turn to the back of the book for the other verses. Then you can try some of the various songs given on pages 17 or those listed here. The chord sequences for some of the songs opposite are given at the back of the book.

ANNIE'S SONG (John Denver)
THE BLACK VELVET BAND (The Dubliners)
BIRD ON A WIRE (Leonard Cohen)
ROCK-A-BYE BABY (Traditional)
I NEVER WILL MARRY (Traditional).

Bass-Chord Style

EXPECTED CHORDS

In much traditional music and simpler modern songs, the only chords used in the accompaniment are those 'expected' in that particular key i.e. the major and minor chords that are made up from notes in the key scale - like the chords you've been using so far, which are all 'expected' in the key of **C** major: **C, Dm, Em, F, G,** & **Am.**

Out-Of-Key Chords

In many songs today, accompaniments are made more interesting by the occasional use of chords that are not 'expected' in the key chosen for the music. These chords are called 'out-of-key' chords because they contain one or more notes that aren't from the key scale - but they can sound fine as long as they're used for a short period and in particular sequences that our ears can accept.

The D (Major) Chord

The key of the next accompaniment, like all the songs so far, is **C** major. The 'expected' **D** chord in this key is **D** *minor*, but a **D** major chord is also used:

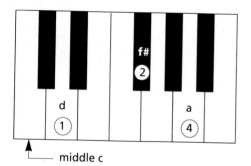

This is your first chance to play a black key - the **f#** (sharp) note. The **f#** is the black key immediately to the right of the **f** (white key) note. Use the same fingering as for the other chords you've learnt so far, but move your whole right hand slightly further in

over the keys as shown - this will make holding the chord a little more comfortable.

Major/Minor Difference

You'll notice that the difference between the **D** minor and **D** major chords is just one note - the **f** note becomes **f#**. The lowered middle note of the major chord creates a 'sadder' sounding minor chord.

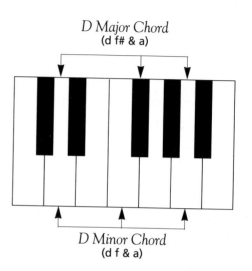

D Major Chord
(d f# & a)

D Minor Chord
(d f & a)

D Major Chord In The Key Of C

In the next song, "It Doesn't Matter Any More", the **D** chord is used after the **C** chord. The **G** chord follows, with the **C** completing the sequence. When the **D** chord is played it creates some tension (because it's an out-of-key chord), but not too much. The tension is resolved when the **G** chord comes along.

This is a kind of 'temporary key change', and is one of the most common in modern music. You'll see it again in two more featured songs in the book - "My Bonnie" and "I Love You Because".

Bass-Chord Style

THE SAME BASS NOTES

The next song, "It Doesn't Matter Any More", involves a 4-beat rhythm with both major and minor chords. To start with, you could play the same bass notes on the 1st and 3rd beats of each bar as you did for "Wooden Heart":

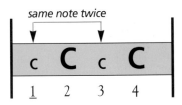

same note twice

When playing just the low root note of each chord, you should hold your left hand as you did before - shown in the diagram below. The little finger ⑤ plays the **c** note for the **C** chord bass, the ring finger ④ the **d** note for **Dm** (or the **D** chord), and so on.

Move your left hand thumb ① along one key to the **a** note for the **Am** chord (as you did for "Try To Remember"):

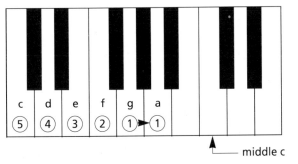

ALTERNATING BASS NOTES

The accompaniment for "It Doesn't Matter Any More" involves alternating bass notes between the right hand chords:

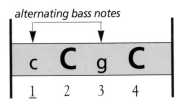

alternating bass notes

Alternating bass notes create more variety in the accompaniment and produce a bouncier rhythm. For the **C** chord, the low **c** note is played on the 1st beat of the bar followed by the right hand **C** chord on the 2nd beat. Then the low **g** note *below* the low **c** is played before the **C** chord on the 4th beat.

Your left hand should be in this position:

Bass Notes for C Chord

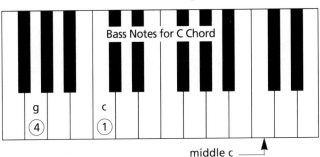

Your left hand thumb ① plays the low **c** note, and the ring finger ④ the **g** even lower. The same left hand fingers are used for the **G** chord notes - move your hand up to the right.

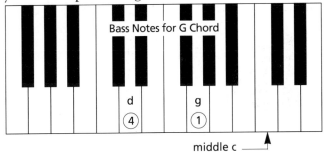

Bass Notes for G Chord

The **a** & **d** bass notes for the **D** chord should be played one key up from the **g** & **c** notes for the **C** chord, and the bass **e** & **a** note for the **Am** chord should be played one key up from the **d** & **g** notes for the **G** chord. Use the same fingers.

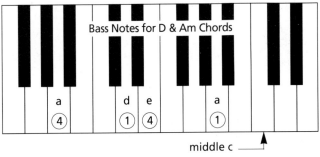

Bass Notes for D & Am Chords

It Doesn't Matter Any More

Go over the sequence for "It Doesn't Matter Any More" very carefully. When you can get through slowly but steadily, try singing as well. Here's the melody, which includes the black key **c#**. This is found to the right of the white **c** key.

There you go and baby here am I
e d c g c d e d c

Well you left me here so I could sit and cry
d e f e d c#d e f e d

Well golly gee what have you done to me?
c d e d c g c d e d c

I guess it doesn't matter any more.
c d d d d b b b c

Middle Section

There's no use in me a-cry-y-in'
a a a b c d e d c

I've done everything and now I'm sick of tryin'
d e e g e d c d e e d c

I've thrown away my nights
c d d d e d

Wasted all my days over you.
d d d e d e d g

BUDDY HOLLY

IT DOESN'T MATTER ANY MORE
Words and Music by Paul Anka

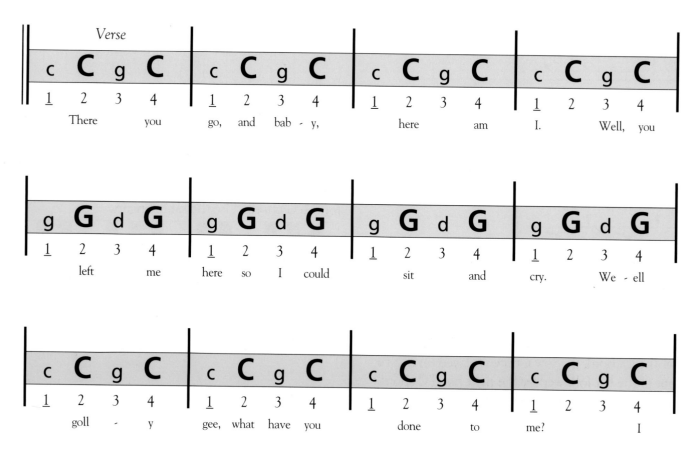

c	**C**	g	**C**	c	**C**	g	**C**	c	**C**	g	**C**	c	**C**	g	**C**
<u>1</u>	2	3	4	<u>1</u>	2	3	4	<u>1</u>	2	3	4	<u>1</u>	2	3	4
There		you		go,	and	bab -	y,		here		am	I.		Well,	you

g	**G**	d	**G**	g	**G**	d	**G**	g	**G**	d	**G**	g	**G**	d	**G**
<u>1</u>	2	3	4	<u>1</u>	2	3	4	<u>1</u>	2	3	4	<u>1</u>	2	3	4
left		me		here	so	I	could		sit		and		cry.		We - ell

c	**C**	g	**C**	c	**C**	g	**C**	c	**C**	g	**C**	c	**C**	g	**C**
<u>1</u>	2	3	4	<u>1</u>	2	3	4	<u>1</u>	2	3	4	<u>1</u>	2	3	4
goll -		y		gee,	what	have	you		done		to		me?		I

IT DOESN'T MATTER ANY MORE
(Continued)

d Dm	a Dm	g G	d G	c C	g C	c C	g C
1 2	3 4	1 2	3 4	1 2	3 4	1 2	3 4

guess it does - n't matt - er an - y more.

Middle Section

a Am	e Am	a Am	e Am	c C	g C	c C	g C
1 2	3 4	1 2	3 4	1 2	3 4	1 2	3 4

There's no use in me a - cry - in'. I've

c C	g C	c C	g C	c C	g C	c C	g C
1 2	3 4	1 2	3 4	1 2	3 4	1 2	3 4

done ev' - ry thing and now I'm sick of try - in'. I've

d D	a D	d D	a D	d D	a D	d D	a D
1 2	3 4	1 2	3 4	1 2	3 4	1 2	3 4

thrown a - way my nights, wast - ed all my days ov - er

g G	d G	g G	d G	g G	d G	g G	d G
1 2	3 4	1 2	3 4	1 2	3 4	1 2	3 4

you.

ADDITIONAL SONGS

The other verses for "It Doesn't Matter Any More" are at the back of the book. When you're ready for more material in the 4-beat alternating bass style, try some of the songs given on page 23, or some of these listed here - they can all be played with the chords you've used so far. The sequences for some of them are given in the back of the book.

WHAT HAVE THEY DONE TO MY SONG, MA? (Melanie)
WHERE I'M BOUND (Tom Paxton)
ACT NATURALLY (Ringo Starr)
COME OUTSIDE (Mike Sarne)
GOOD LUCK CHARM (Elvis Presley)
WHISKEY IN THE JAR (Traditional)
BANKS OF THE OHIO (Traditional).

Arpeggio Style

CHORD ARPEGGIOS

Chord notes can be played one after the other instead of all at the same time. This is called a chord arpeggio. Try playing an arpeggio of the **C** chord, using the same right hand fingers as usual:

```
c   e   g   c   e   g   c   e   g   c   e   g
①  ②  ④  ①  ②  ④  ①  ②  ④  ①  ②  ④
```

Play the **c**, **e** & **g** notes from left to right and repeat them over and over again until you can play them smoothly and steadily. Keep the correct fingers over the notes so as little movement as possible is necessary. Now try playing the **C** chord notes up and *back* again, like this:

```
c   e   g   e   c
①  ②  ④  ②  ①
```

3-BEAT ARPEGGIO PATTERN

Chord arpeggios can be used to create a different and effective keyboard style. Try playing this simple 3-beat arpeggio pattern which is used for the next song, "My Bonnie":

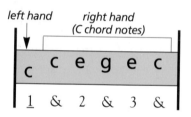

Play the low **c** root note with the little finger ⑤ of your left hand - on the 1st beat - then the right hand **C** chord notes as shown.

Notes Between Beats

For simplicity, you've played notes and chords only *on* the beat so far. Arpeggio patterns involve notes on and off the beat. Count the patterns as indicated, tapping your foot on each beat. The notes between beats must be played *exactly halfway* between the beats. Stress the 1st beat of the bar as usual, but also stress the other beat notes slightly more than the notes off the beat. Play the pattern over and over till you produce a flowing and steady rhythm.

Left Hand Notes

The arpeggio patterns for the other chords in "My Bonnie" involve a similar sequence and finger movement - starting with the chord root note by the left hand. *Each chord is indicated above the notation.* The low notes are played by the same left hand fingers used on page 20 (**d** is played by your ring finger ④, so your hand stays in the same position).

My Bonnie

Here's the first line of "My Bonnie" with the melody notes - I'm sure you can take it from there!

My Bonnie lies over the ocean
g e d c d c a g e

MY BONNIE
Traditional, arranged by Russ Shipton

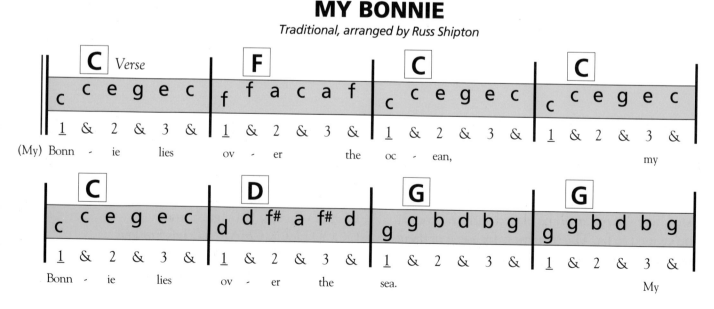

MY BONNIE
(Continued)

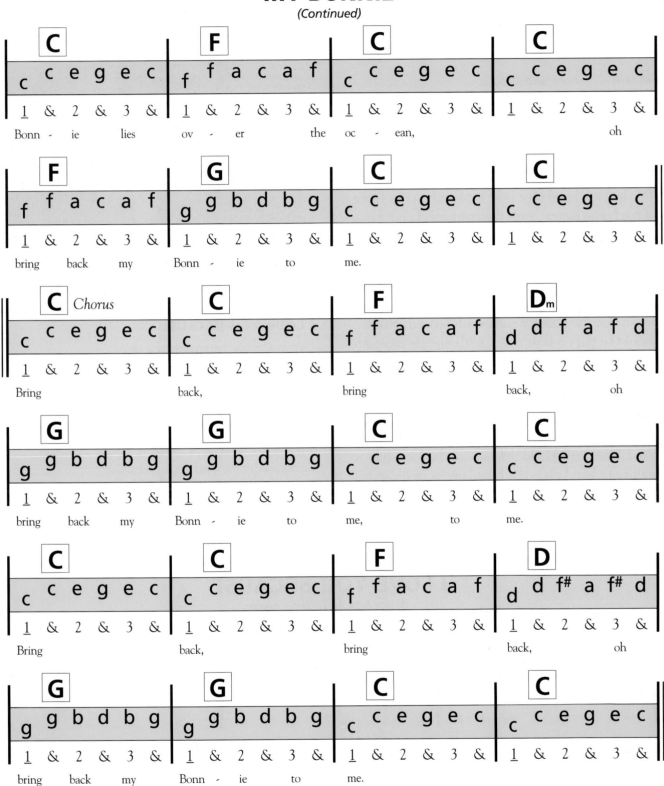

ADDITIONAL SONGS

When you've mastered "My Bonnie", have a go at
playing some other 3-beat songs in the arpeggio style.
Choose some from those listed on pages 9, 11, 17 & 25.

4-BEAT ARPEGGIO PATTERN

To produce a 4-beat arpeggio pattern, two notes can be added to the simple 3-beat pattern that you used for "My Bonnie":

JIM REEVES

left hand   *right hand (C chord)*

C	c	e	g	e	c	e	g
	1	&	2	&	3	&	4	&

The low left hand root note is played on the 1st beat of the bar as before, with the right hand chord notes used for the rest of the pattern. This time you move up the chord, back down again, then up again - use the same fingers i.e. ①, ② & ④.

Count the bar carefully, and play the notes smoothly. Make sure the notes are all evenly spaced. Stress should be put on beat notes, with slightly more stress on the 1st beat note.

Length of Notes

In the arpeggio style notes should not be stopped - they should be held for a full half beat. The low left hand note can be held throughout the bar while your right hand plays the chord notes, or it can be held for a shorter time - experiment!

I Love You Because

I love you because you understand dear
g c e g c e d c a c

Every single thing I try to do
g g f# g c a g e d

You're always there to lend a helping hand dear
b c c e g c e d c a c

I love you most of all because you're you
a g g c a b c d d c

No matter what the world may say about me
c c a a b c b d c a g

I know your love will always see me through.
g f# f f# g a a d c b

(Melody of ending is the same as lines 3 &4)

I LOVE YOU BECAUSE
Words & Music by Leon Payne

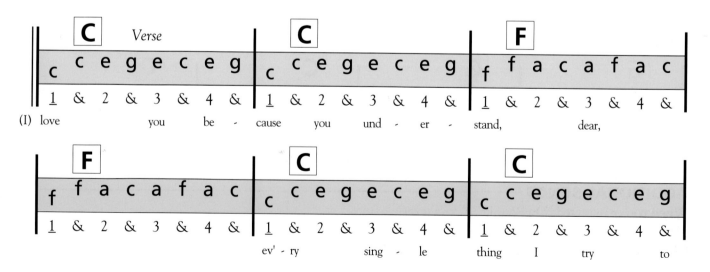

32

Arpeggio Style

I LOVE YOU BECAUSE
(Continued)

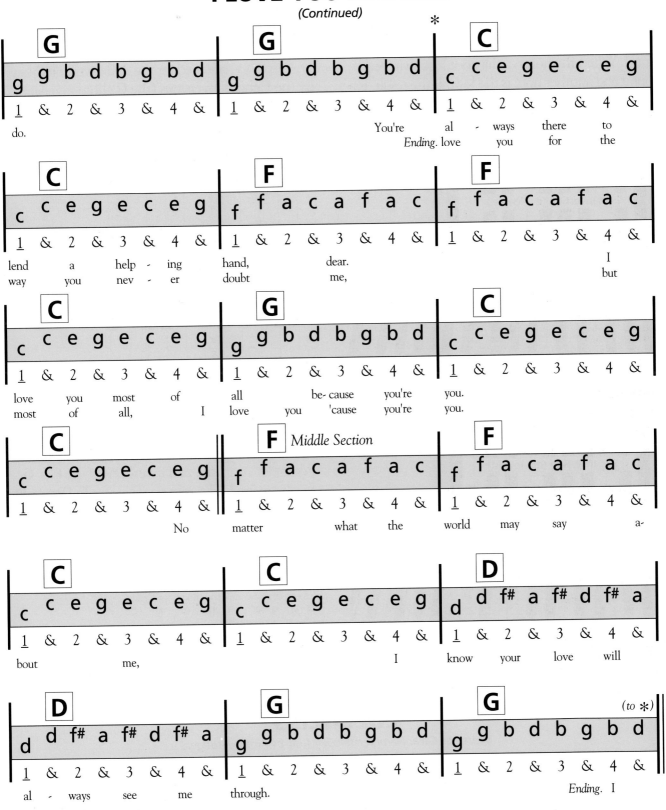

- choose the ballads from those on pages 13, 15 & 19.

ADDITIONAL SONGS

Now try playing other 4-beat songs in the arpeggio style
- choose the ballads from those on pages 13, 15 & 19.

CHORD INVERSIONS

So far - to keep things simple - you've used right hand chords in their basic form, known as the 'root position' (where the root of the chord is the lowest note). When the notes of the chord are switched round and another note is the lowest, the result is a 'chord inversion'. Inversions are important because they can allow quicker finger movement and smoother chord progressions. Try the two inversions of the **C** chord:

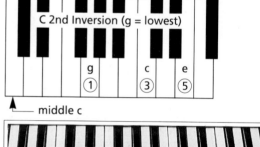

C 1st Inversion (e = lowest)

e ① g ② c ⑤

— middle c

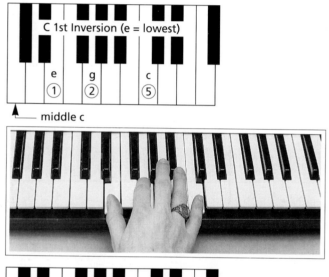

C 2nd Inversion (g = lowest)

g ① c ③ e ⑤

— middle c

The fingering changes for the inversions because the spread of the keys changes. The thumb, index and little finger ①, ② & ⑤ are used for the 1st inversion, while the thumb, middle and little finger ①, ③ & ⑤ are used for the 2nd inversion. Now try the **F** chord inversions (the **G** chord inversions are one key up from these):

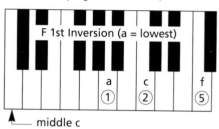

F 1st Inversion (a = lowest)

a ① c ② f ⑤

— middle c

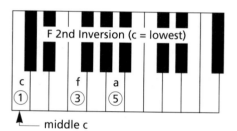

F 2nd Inversion (c = lowest)

c ① f ③ a ⑤

— middle c

Edelweiss

Depending on the sound you want and the ease of fingering, only *some* inversions may be necessary. In "Edelweiss", only the 2nd inversions of the **F** & **G** chords are used. The root positions for **C**, **Dm** & **D** are played.

Edelweiss, Edelweiss, every morning you greet me
e g d c g f e e e f g a g

Small and white, clean and bright, you look happy to meet me.
  e g d c g f   e g g a b c c

Blossom of snow may you bloom and grow
  d g g b a g e g c

Bloom and grow forever.
  a c d c b g

EDELWEISS

Words by Oscar Hammerstein II, Music by Richard Rodgers

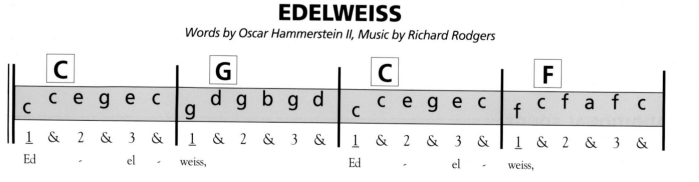

C						G						C						F					
c	c e g e c					g	d g b g d					c	c e g e c					f	c f a f c				
1	&	2	&	3	&	1	&	2	&	3	&	1	&	2	&	3	&	1	&	2	&	3	&
Ed	-		el	-	weiss,							Ed	-		el	-	weiss,						

Arpeggio Style

EDELWEISS
(Continued)

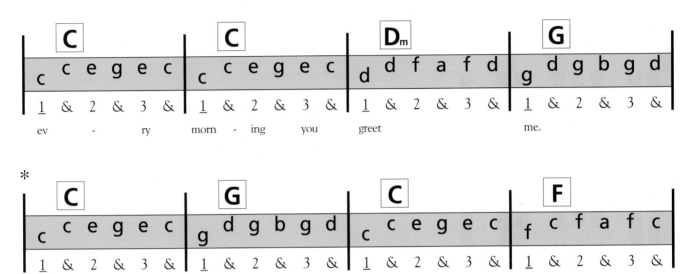

C	**C**	**D**m	**G**
c c e g e c	c c e g e c	d d f a f d	g d g b g d
1 & 2 & 3 &	1 & 2 & 3 &	1 & 2 & 3 &	1 & 2 & 3 &
ev - ry morn - ing you	greet		me.

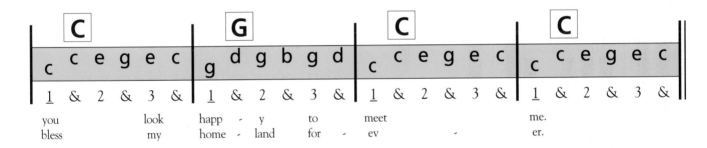

*

C	**G**	**C**	**F**
c c e g e c	g d g b g d	c c e g e c	f c f a f c
1 & 2 & 3 &	1 & 2 & 3 &	1 & 2 & 3 &	1 & 2 & 3 &
Small and white,		clean and bright,	

Ending. Ed - el - weiss,   Ed - el - weiss,

C	**G**	**C**	**C**
c c e g e c	g d g b g d	c c e g e c	c c e g e c
1 & 2 & 3 &	1 & 2 & 3 &	1 & 2 & 3 &	1 & 2 & 3 &
you look happ - y to meet			me.

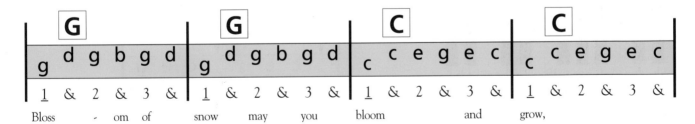

you look happ - y to meet me.
bless my home - land for - ev - er.

G	**G**	**C**	**C**
g d g b g d	g d g b g d	c c e g e c	c c e g e c
1 & 2 & 3 &	1 & 2 & 3 &	1 & 2 & 3 &	1 & 2 & 3 &
Bloss - om of snow may you	bloom and grow,		

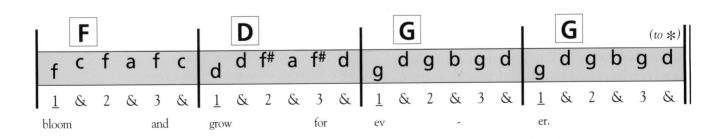

F	**D**	**G**	**G** (to *)
f c f a f c	d d f# a f# d	g d g b g d	g d g b g d
1 & 2 & 3 &	1 & 2 & 3 &	1 & 2 & 3 &	1 & 2 & 3 &
bloom and grow for ev - er.			

ADDITIONAL SONGS

Now try experimenting with the arrangements of some
previous 3-beat songs by including inversions.

MINOR CHORD INVERSIONS

As you've seen, the three 'expected' minor chords in the key of **C** major are **Dm**, **Em** & **Am**. You need to know the inversions of these chords as well as those for the major chords:

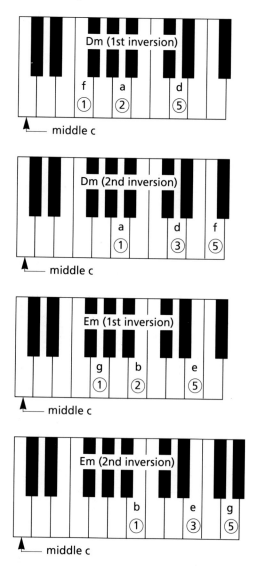

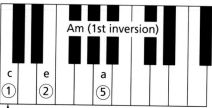

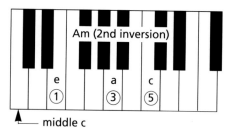

The fingering is the same as that for the major chord inversions.

Notice that the 1st & 2nd inversions of the **Am** chord can be played nearer **middle c** than the root position - like the 2nd inversion of the **F** chord. Generally it's better to play notes round the middle of the keyboard when accompanying songs, then the sound won't be too low or too shrill.

ANOTHER 4-BEAT PATTERN

Bars 7 & 15 in the accompaniment for "In The Bleak Midwinter" involve *two* chords instead of the usual one. **F** is played for two beats and **G** for two beats. Here you play the low root of the chord with the left hand, followed by just the three notes of the chord once through.

When you've played through the accompaniment for "In The Bleak Midwinter", you could try using this kind of 'two to the bar' pattern all the way through:

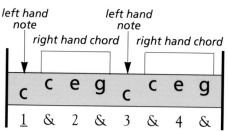

In The Bleak Midwinter

In the bleak midwinter, frosty wind made moan
e f g   e d c d e d   a d

Earth stood hard as iron, water like a stone
 e   f   g e d c d e d c c

Snow had fallen snow on snow, snow on snow
  f   e f g a a e g e d c   d

In the bleak midwinter, long ago.
e f g   e d c d e d c c

Arpeggio Style

IN THE BLEAK MIDWINTER

Words by Christina Rosetti, Music by Ferdinand Holtz, arranged by Russ Shipton

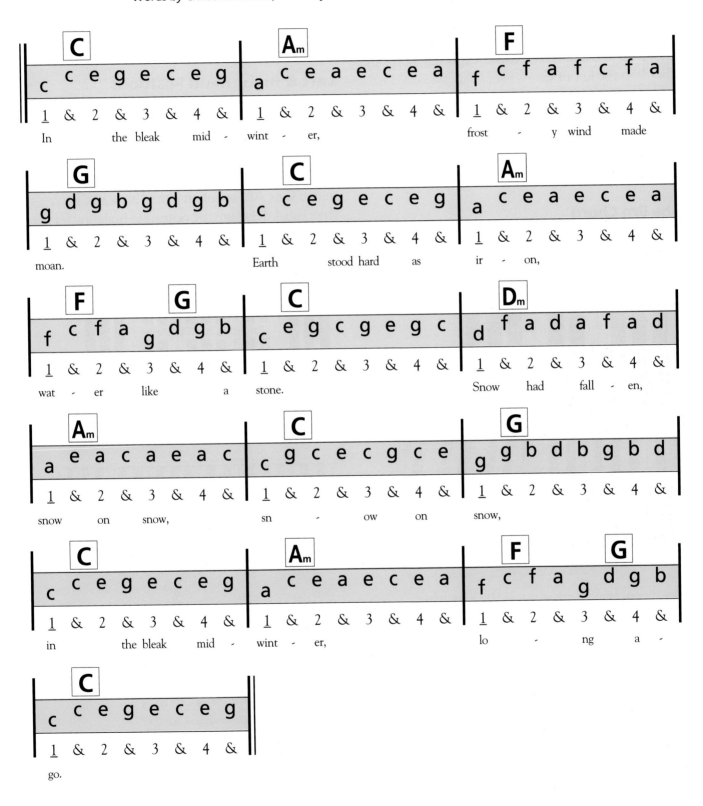

ADDITIONAL SONGS

Now try including inversions in previous 4-beat accompaniments.

ANOTHER KEY: G MAJOR

Different keys are needed to match the singer's vocal range. The key of G major is used for the last two songs in Book 1, which means the melody should end on g note and the accompaniment on a G chord. Here is a summary of the 'expected' notes and chords in the key of G:

Notes g a b c d e f#

Chords G Am Bm C D Em

You've seen all the chords already, apart from Bm.

The Bm Chord

The Bm chord is fingered like the other chords you know. Like the D major chord, it includes a black key note, f#:

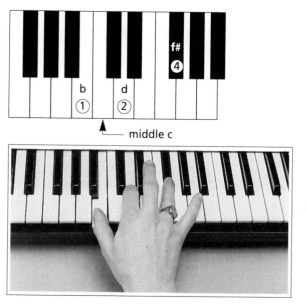

Move your hand further across the keys when playing the Bm chord, as shown in the photo.

ANOTHER 3-BEAT PATTERN

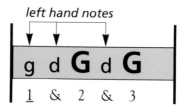

left hand notes

g d **G** d **G**

1 & 2 & 3

This pattern is a variation on the 3-beat pattern you've seen already. It's a sort of cross between the bass-chord and arpeggio styles. The left hand little

finger ⑤ begins the pattern with a low g note followed by a d note played with the thumb ①. The right hand then plays a G chord on the 2nd beat. The left hand plays a d note again and the right hand ends the pattern with another chord.

Left & Right Hand Positions

The little finger ⑤ then thumb ① of the left hand always play the two low notes of each chord pattern- *all* played below middle c. The right hand chords, apart from G & Am, are played in the usual positions, using the root form. In the new key of G major, G & Am are often played an *octave lower* than usual. Here are the notes and fingering for the G chord pattern - for both hands. The same fingering is used for the Am chord pattern, just one key to the right:

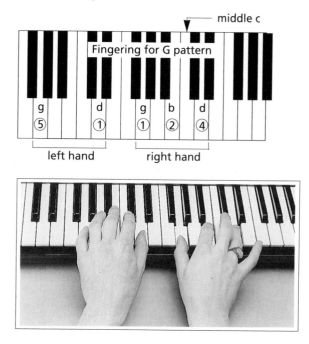

The Mountains Of Mourne

Oh Mary this London's a wonderful sight
d db b b a g a g g

With people here working by day and by night
e e d d d e f# a g g

(Lines 3 & 4 have the same melody as lines 1 & 2)

At least when I asked them that's what I was told
d d c c c d c c b a b

So I just took a hand at this diggin' for gold
b a g b d d c b b a g a

But for all that I found there I might as well be
d d d b g b a g g a b c

Where the mountains of Mourne sweep down to the sea.
e e e d d de f# a g g

Arpeggio Style

THE MOUNTAINS OF MOURNE

Traditional, arranged by Russ Shipton

g d **G** d **G**	g d **G** d **G**	c g **C** g **C**	a e **A**m e **A**m
1 & 2 & 3	1 & 2 & 3	1 & 2 & 3	1 & 2 & 3

Oh) Ma - ry this Lon - don's a wond - er - ful sight, with
don't sow pot - at - oes, nor bar - ley nor wheat, but there's

(Repeat 8 bars)

d a **D** a **D**	d a **D** a **D**	c g **C** g **C**	g d **G** d **G**
1 & 2 & 3	1 & 2 & 3	1 & 2 & 3	1 & 2 & 3

peo - ple here work - ing by day and by night. They/
gangs of them diggin' for gold in the street. At

d a **D** a **D**	d a **D** a **D**	e b **E**m b **E**m	e b **E**m b **E**m
1 & 2 & 3	1 & 2 & 3	1 & 2 & 3	1 & 2 & 3

least when I asked them that's what I was told, so I

g d **G** d **G**	b f# **B**m f# **B**m	a e **A**m e **A**m	d a **D** a **D**
1 & 2 & 3	1 & 2 & 3	1 & 2 & 3	1 & 2 & 3

just took a hand at this diggin' for gold. But for

g d **G** d **G**	g d **G** d **G**	c g **C** g **C**	a e **A**m e **A**m
1 & 2 & 3	1 & 2 & 3	1 & 2 & 3	1 & 2 & 3

all that I found there, I might as well be where the

d a **D** a **D**	d a **D** a **D**	c g **C** g **C**	g d **G** d **G**
1 & 2 & 3	1 & 2 & 3	1 & 2 & 3	1 & 2 & 3

mount - ains of Mou - rne sweep down to the sea.

Note: You can make this 3-beat pattern a 4-beat one by playing the
last note and chord again. Try using these new patterns for
previous songs.

4-BEAT RHYTHM PATTERN

The next song involves a variation on the bass-chord pattern you learnt earlier. This one is suitable for pop songs with a steady and driving rhythm, like "The Loco-motion":

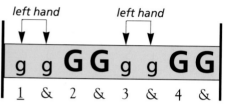

The left hand plays two low **g** notes, followed by the right hand with two **G** chords. This is repeated for the other half of the bar.

Another Chord: A (Major)

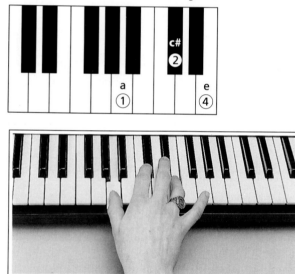

As you've seen, the **D** major chord is sometimes used

in the key of **C** - where it is an out-of-key chord. In the key of **G**, the equivalent out-of-key chord is **A** major, which involves one black key note, **c#**.

Left & Right Hand Positions

The **C** & **D** chords are played as before. The other chords (**G, Em, Am** & **A**) are played an *octave lower than usual*. So you can concentrate on the new pattern, use root positions for all the chords.

For the left hand, the low notes match the chords i.e. one octave lower for **G, Em, Am** & **A**. ① & ③ are used for **G** & **Em** at the start, and also for the **C** & **Am/A** bars that follow. ⑤ is used for the next **G** bars, ① for **D** then ⑤ for the **G** bars afterwards. Try to use no more movement than necessary.

The Loco-motion

Everybody's doin' a brand new dance now
g a g a b a g d e   d   e   g

Come on baby, do the locomotion
 d   d d d e e   e e e e

(Lines 3 & 4 have the same melody as lines 1 & 2)

My little baby sister can do it with ease
o c d c d e d c g a a g   a

It's easier than learnin' your A B C's
g e d c d   e d c g b a g

So come on, come on, do the locomotion with me.
g e d   b   g a a b a b a   b g

You gotta swing your hips now
 g b d e   d   b g

Come on baby, jump up, jump back
 b   a g a e d b   g

Oh well I think you got the knack.
g b   d e d   d   e   d

THE LOCO-MOTION

Words & Music by Gerry Goffin & Carole King

g	g	**G** **G**	g	g	**G** **G**	e	e	**E**ₘ **E**ₘ	e	e	**E**ₘ **E**ₘ	g	g	**G** **G**	g	g	**G** **G**
1	&	2 &	3	&	4 &	1	&	2 &	3	&	4 &	1	&	2 &	3	&	4 &

Ev'-ry bod-y's do - in' a brand   new dance   now.   Come on   bab-y,   do

e	e	**E**ₘ **E**ₘ	e	e	**E**ₘ **E**ₘ	g	g	**G** **G**	g	g	**G** **G**	e	e	**E**ₘ **E**ₘ	e	e	**E**ₘ **E**ₘ
1	&	2 &	3	&	4 &	1	&	2 &	3	&	4 &	1	&	2 &	3	&	4 &

the loc - o - mot - ion. I know you'll get to like it if you give it a chance   now.

40

THE LOCO-MOTION

(Continued)

g	g	**G**	**G**	g	g	**G**	**G**	e	e	**Eₘ**	**Eₘ**	e	e	**Eₘ**	**Eₘ**	c	c	**C**	**C**	c	c	**C**	**C**
1	&	2	&	3	&	4	&	1	&	2	&	3	&	4	&	1	&	2	&	3	&	4	&

Come on   bab - y,   do   the loc - o - mot - ion. My litt - le bab - y sis - ter can

a	a	**Aₘ**	**Aₘ**	a	a	**Aₘ**	**Aₘ**	c	c	**C**	**C**	c	c	**C**	**C**	a	a	**A**	**A**	a	a	**A**	**A**
1	&	2	&	3	&	4	&	1	&	2	&	3	&	4	&	1	&	2	&	3	&	4	&

do it with ease.   It's eas - i - er than lear - nin' your A   B -   C's,   so

g	g	**G**	**G**	g	g	**G**	**G**	d	d	**D**	**D**	d	d	**D**	**D**	g	g	**G**	**G**	g	g	**G**	**G**
1	&	2	&	3	&	4	&	1	&	2	&	3	&	4	&	1	&	2	&	3	&	4	&

come on,   come on,   do   the loc - o - mot - ion with   me.   You got - ta

g	g	**G**	**G**	g	g	**G**	**G**	c	c	**C**	**C**	c	c	**C**	**C**	c	c	**C**	**C**	c	c	**C**	**C**
1	&	2	&	3	&	4	&	1	&	2	&	3	&	4	&	1	&	2	&	3	&	4	&

swing   your   hips   now.   Come on   bab - y,   jump up,

g	g	**G**	**G**	g	g	**G**	**G**	g	g	**G**	**G**	g	g	**G**	**G**	d	d	**D**	**D**	d	d	**D**	**D**
1	&	2	&	3	&	4	&	1	&	2	&	3	&	4	&	1	&	2	&	3	&	4	&

jump back.   Oh well I think   you   got   the

d	d	**D**	**D**	d	d	**D**	**D**
1	&	2	&	3	&	4	&

knack.

ADDITIONAL SONGS

You can use the same rock pattern for these other rock and pop songs (the chord sequences for some of them are in the back of the book).

SWEETS FOR MY SWEET (The Searchers)
HANG ON SLOOPY (The McCoys)
LET'S TWIST AGAIN (Chubby Checker)
CROCODILE ROCK (Elton John)
DREAM LOVER (Bobby Darin)
SUGARTIME (The McGuire Sisters).

Additional Practice Songs

Note: 1 CHORD SYMBOL=1 BAR OR PATTERN

C
1   2   3

Page 9

THE JOYS OF LOVE

Verse 2

```
        C    G    C  C
When your lips kissed mine
F       C       G  G
I felt a love divine
 F   G      C          F
You gave me heaven on earth
        C    G    C  C
When your lips kissed mine.
```

Verse 3

```
         C      G        C C
The skies were always blue
           F     C          G G
When I could call you my own
            F   G       C
The wind has brought the clouds
        F    C   G     C C
To rain on me now you are gone.
```

AMAZING GRACE
C	C	F	C
C	C	G	G
C	C	F	C
C	G	C	C

HOME ON THE RANGE
C	C	F	F
C	C	G	G
C	C	F	F

1st Line Chorus
C	G	C	C

HAPPY BIRTHDAY TO YOU
C	G	G	C
C	F	C	C

SO LONG, IT'S BEEN GOOD TO KNOW YOU
C	C	C	C
G	G	C	C
C	C	F	F
C	G	C	C

C   C   C
1   2   3

Page 11

BACHELOR BOY

Verse 3

```
C          C        F     F      G
When I was sixteen I fell in love with a girl
 G            C C
As sweet as could be
C       C        F     F
But I remembered just in time
              G   G    C G
What my daddy said to me, he said:
```

Verse 4 (same as verse 2)

Verse 5

```
C           C    F        F
As time goes by I probably will
G    G       C    C
Meet a girl and fall in love
C          C         F        F
Then I'll get married have a wife and a child
   G       G    C
Any they'll be my turtle doves.
```

Verse 6

```
  G         C C     F      F
But until then I'll be a bachelor boy
    G       G     C C
And that's the way I'll stay
C         C  F        F    G   G    C
Happy to be a bachelor boy until my dyin' day.
```

CLEMENTINE
C	C	G	G
F	C	G	C

AWAY IN A MANGER
C	C	C	F
F	C	F	G
C	C	C	F
F	C	G	C

LAVENDER BLUE
C	C	F	F
C	C	G	C

C
1   2   3   4

Page 13

THE SLOOP JOHN B.

Verse 2

```
             C            C
Well the first mate he got drunk
              C             C
And destroyed the people's trunk
             C              C        G G
And constable come aboard, take him away
                     C  C            F F
Now Sheriff Johnstone, please let me alone
  C            G            C C
I feel so broke up, I wanna go home.
```

Verse 3

```
             C             C
Well the poor cook he got the fits
    C          C
Threw away all the grits
    C            C         G G
Then he took and eat all of my corn
            C  C          F F
Let me go home, I wanna go home
     C             G         C C
Oh this is the worst trip since I was born.
```

THE LAST THING ON MY MIND
C	F	C	F	C	G	C	C
C	F	C	F	C	G	C	C

Chorus
C	G	C	G	C	C	C	G
C	F	C	C	G	G	C	C

HUSH LITTLE BABY
C	G	G	C
C	G	G	C

TOM DOOLEY
C	C	C	G
G	G	G	C

ROCK AROUND THE CLOCK
C	C	C	C
C	C	G	G

Other Verse
C	C	C	C
F	F	C	C
G	G	C	C

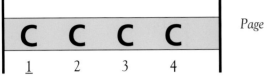

C	C	C	C		*Page 15*
<u>1</u>	2	3	4		

D_m	D_m	D_m		*Page 17*
<u>1</u>	2	3		

DA DOO RON RON

Verse 2

  C   F
Knew what he was doing when he caught my eye
  G   C
Da doo ron ron ron, da doo ron ron
  C   F
He looked so good he was oh my oh my
  G   C
Da doo ron ron ron, da doo ron ron
C   F   C   G
Yeah he caught my eye, yeah oh my oh my
C
And when he walked me home   F
  G   C
Da doo ron ron ron, da doo ron ron.

Verse 3

  C   F
Picked me up at seven and he looked so fine
  G   C
Da doo ron ron ron, da doo ron ron
  C   F
One day soon I'm gonna make him mine
  G   C
Da doo ron ron ron, da doo ron ron
C   F   C   G
Yeah he looked so fine, yeah gonna make him mine
C   F
And when he walked me home
  G   C
Da doo ron ron ron, da doo ron ron.

THE RIDDLE SONG

C	F	F	C
G	C	C	G
G	C	C	G
C	F	F	C

AULD LANG SYNE

C	G	C	F
C	G	C/G	C
Chorus			
C	C	F	F
C	G	C	G

GREEN GREEN GRASS OF HOME

C	C	F	C
C	C	G	G
C	C	F	F
C	G	C	G

HEARTBREAK HOTEL

C	C	C	C
F	C	G	C

> *Note:* C/G = 2 BEATS PER CHORD

SILENT NIGHT

Verse 2

  C   C   C   C
Silent night, holy night
  G   G   C   C
Shepherds quake at the sight
  F   F   C   C
Glories stream from heaven afar
  F   F   C   C
Heavenly hosts sing allelujah
  Dm   G   C Am
Christ the saviour is born
  C   G   C   C
Christ the saviour is born.

OH DEAR, WHAT CAN THE MATTER BE?

C	G	C	C
Dm	Dm	G	G
C	G	C	C
Dm	G	C	C
Chorus			
C	C	C	C
C	G	G	G
C	C	C	C
Dm	G	C	C

IN DUBLIN'S FAIR CITY

C	Am	Dm	G
C	C	F	G
C	Am	Dm	G
C	Am	G	C

THE NIGHTINGALE

C	C	G	C
C	C	C	G
C	C	G	G
C	F	G	C
Chorus			
C	F	G	C
C	Am	Dm	G
C	C	C	G
C	F	G	C

IT'S FOUR IN THE MORNING

C	C	C	C	C	C	Dm	G
G	G	G	G	G	G	C	C
C	C	C	C	C	C	F	F
F	G	C	Am	F	G	C	C

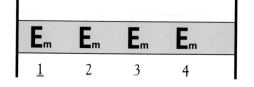

Page 19

Page 21

A GROOVY KIND OF LOVE

Verse 2

```
G                    C                          G
Any time you want to you can turn me on to
                     C                 G
Anything you want to any time at all
                     Dm               Em
When I taste your lips, oh I start to shiver
                         Dm / F     G
Can't control the quivering inside (etc.)
```

Verse 3

```
G                    C                          G
Any time you want to you can turn me on to
                     C                 G
Anything you want to any time at all
                     Dm                     Em
When I'm in your arms, nothing seems to matter
                       Dm / F       G
If the world would shatter, I don't care (etc.)
```

THE ROSE

```
C    G    F/G   C
C    G    F/G   C
C    F    F     G
C    G    F     C
C    G    F/G   C
C    G    F/G   C
Am   Dm   F     G
C    G    F/G   C
```

THE LEAVING OF LIVERPOOL

```
C    F/G   C     C
C    F/G   C/G   C
```
Chorus
```
G    F/C   Am/Em Dm/G
C    F/C
```

THE WATER IS WIDE

```
C    F    C    C
Am   F    G    G
Em   Em   Am   Am
C    G    C    C
```

WHERE HAVE ALL THE FLOWERS GONE?

```
C    Am   F    G
C    Am   Dm   G
C    Am   F    G
F    C    F    G
C    Am   F    G
```

THE WILD ROVER

Verse 2

```
           C         C         C          F    F
I went to the alehouse I used to frequent
           C       G       G            C
And I told the landlady my money was spent
           C         C            C         F    F
I asked her for credit and she answered me "Nay"
         C        G       G          C
"Such custom as yours I could have every day".
```

Verse 3

```
           C          C         C          F    F
I took out from my pocket ten sovereigns bright
           C          G       G          C
And the landlady's eyes opened wide with delight
           C        C          C         F    F
She said "I have whiskies and wines of the best"
          C        G         G          C
"And the words that you told me were only in jest".
```

Verse 4

```
           C         C          C         F    F
I'll go home to my parents, confess what I've done
          C        G       G          C
And I'll ask them to pardon their prodigal son
            C          C          C          F    F
And when they've caressed me as oft times before
         C        G        C
I never will play the wild rover no more.
```

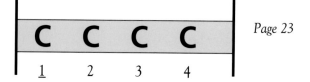

Page 23

WOODEN HEART

Verse 3

```
                 C              G
Treat me nice, treat me good
                 C              C
Treat me like you really should
              C             C
'Cause I'm not made of wood
              G        G    C    C
And I don't have a wooden heart
```

TRAVELIN' LIGHT				YOU'RE MY BEST FRIEND				THIS TRAIN			
C	C	C	C	C	G	C	C	C	C	C	C
F	F	C	C	F	F	C	C	C	C	G	G
G	G	C	C	C	C	F	F	C	C	F	F
F	G	C	C	C	G	C	C	C	G	C	.C
Middle Section				C	F	C	C				
F	F	C	C	G	G	C	C				
F	F	G	G	C	C	F	F				
G	G			C	G	C	G				

44

Additional Practice Songs

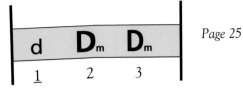

Page 25

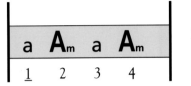

Page 29

TRY TO REMEMBER

Verse 2

```
    C        C            Dm        G
Try to remember when life was so tender
        C         C        Dm     G
That  no one wept except the willow
    C        C            Dm        G
Try to remember when life was so tender
          C        C         Dm    G
That dreams were kept beside your pillow
  Em        Am           Dm     G
Try to remember when life was so tender
          C        F         Dm    G
That love was an ember about to billow
    C        C        Dm     G          C     C Dm G
Try to remember and if you remember, then follow.
```

Verse 3

```
    C          C           Dm        G
Deep in December, it's nice to remember
      C          C         Dm      G
Although you know the snow will follow
    C          C           Dm        G
Deep in December, it's nice to remember
        C         C         Dm   G
Without a hurt, the heart is hollow
  Em        Am           Dm     G
Deep in December, it's nice to remember
        C         F         Dm    G
The fire of September that made us mellow
    C          C           Dm        G
Deep in December, our hearts should remember
        C      C Dm G C
And follow . . .
```

I NEVER WILL MARRY

```
C   G   C   C
F   G   C   C
F   G   C   Am
Dm  G   C   C
```

Chorus

```
G   G   G   G
C   C   C   C
F   F   G   G
C   F   C   G
```

THE BLACK VELVET BAND

```
C   C   C   C
F   F   G   G
C   C   C   Am
Dm  G   C   C
```

ROCK-A-BYE BABY

```
C   C   C   C
C   C   C   C
C   G   F   Dm
G   G   G   C
```

IT DOESN'T MATTER ANY MORE

Verse 2

```
C                    C          C          C
Do you remember, baby, last September
        G           G           G        G
How you held me tight each and every night?
C              C          C            C
Well, oh baby, how you drove me crazy
        Dm          G           C  C
I guess it doesn't matter any more.
```

Verse 3

```
C              C          C         C
Now you go your way, and I'll go mine
G           G           G         G
Now and forever till the end of time
        C            C          C           C
I'll find somebody new and baby we'll say we're thru'
        Dm          G           C  C
And you won't matter any more.
```

GOOD LUCK CHARM

```
C   F   C   G
C   F   G   C
G   G   C   C
G   G   D   G
C   G
```

THE BANKS OF THE OHIO

```
C   C   G   G
G   G   C   C
C   C   F   F
C   G   C   C
```

WHAT HAVE THEY DONE TO MY SONG, MA?

```
C   C   Am  Am
F   F   F   F
C   D   F   F
C   G   C   G
```

WHISKEY IN THE JAR

```
C   C   Am  Am
F   F   C   Am
C   C   Am  Am
F   F   C   Am/F
```

Chorus

```
G   G   C/C  C
F   F   G    C
```

45

Page 31

MY BONNIE

Verse 2

```
   C            F         C    C
Oh blow ye winds over the ocean
   C          D      G    G
And blow ye winds over the sea
   C            F         C    C
Oh blow ye winds over the ocean
        F          G      C  C
And bring back my Bonnie to me.
```

Verse 3

```
       C            F       C    C
Last night as I lay on my pillow
       C          D      G    G
Last night as I lay on my bed
       C            F       C    C
Last night as I lay on my pillow
       F          G       C     C
I dreamed my poor Bonnie was dead.
```

Verse 4

```
    C              F        C    C
The winds have blown over the ocean
    C            D      G    G
The winds have blown over the sea
    C              F        C    C
The winds have blown over the ocean
        F            G     C    C
And brought back my Bonnie to me.
```

Page 37

IN THE BLEAK MIDWINTER

Verse 2

```
   C                Am       F              G
Angels and archangels may have gathered there
   C              Am     F/G         C
Cherubim and Seraphim throng the air
        Dm        Am    C             G
But only his mother in her maiden bliss
   C              Am   F/G      C
Worshipped the beloved with a kiss.
```

Verse3

```
   C           Am        F       G
What can I give him, poor as I am?
   C        Am      F  /   G      C
If I were a shepherd, I would bring a lamb
   Dm        Am       C         G
If I were a wise man, I would do my part
   C            Am     F/G       C
Yet what can I give him, give my heart.
```

Page 39

THE MOUNTAINS OF MOURNE

Verse 2

```
        G              G         C        Am
I believe that when writing a wish you expressed
        D          D       C          G
As to how the fine ladies of London were dressed
        G          G            C        Am
Well if you believe me, when asked to a ball
        D        D         C        G
They don't wear a top to their dresses at all
          D          D       Em          Em
Oh I've seen them myself and you could not in truth
        G          Bm        Am        D
Say if they were bound for a ball or a bath
          G            G          C        Am
Don't be startin' them fashions now Mary Macree
        D            D          C          G
Where the mountains of Mourne sweep down to the sea.
```

Verse 3

```
        G            G          C        Am
There's beautiful girls here, oh never you mind
        D          D        C        G
With beautiful shapes nature never designed
        G            G       C        Am
And lovely complexions, all roses and cream
        D          D        C        G
But I would remark with regard to the same
        D          D        Em        Em
That if at those roses you venture to sip
```

Page 33 box:

```
  C  c e g e c e g
  1 & 2 & 3 & 4 &
```

Page 33

I LOVE YOU BECAUSE

Verse 2

```
   C          C          F      F
I love you because my heart is lighter
C            C            G  G
Every time I'm walking by your side
   C          C            F      F
I love you because the future's brighter
   C          G            C  C
The door to happiness you open wide.
```

Middle Section (2)

```
      F              F         C  C
No matter what may be the style or season
   D            D        G  G
I know your heart will always be true
   C          C            F      F
I love you for a hundred thousand reasons
      C        G              C  C
But most of all I love you 'cause you're you.
```

Additional Practice Songs

```
G              Bm        Am        D
The colours might all come away on your lip
       G        G            C         Am
So I'll wait for the wild rose that's waiting for me
     D       D           C         G
Where the mountains of Mourne sweep down to the sea.
```

```
┌─────────────────────────────────┐
│  g  g  G G  g  g  G G            │   Page 41
├─────────────────────────────────┤
│  1  &  2  &  3  &  4  &          │
└─────────────────────────────────┘
```

THE LOCOMOTION

Verse 2
```
   G                     Em
Now that you can do it, let's make  chain now
G                      Em
Come on baby, do the loco-motion
   G                           Em
A chug-a-chug-a motion like a railroad train now
G                      Em
Come on baby, do the loco-motion
   C                       Am
Do it nice and easy now, don't lose control
   C                          A
A little bit of rhythm and a lot of soul
G                  D                     G
Come on, come on, do the loco-motion with me.
```

Verse 3
```
   G                     Em
Move around the floor in a loco-motion
G                      Em
Come on baby, do the loco-motion
   G                       Em
Do it holding hands if you get the notion
G                      Em
Come on baby, do the locomotion
         C                         Am
There's never been a dance that's so easy to do
   C                              A
It even makes you happy when you're feeling blue
G                  D                     G
So come on, come on, do the loco-motion with me.
```

DREAM LOVER
```
G      G      Em     Em
G      G      Em     Em
G      D      G      C
G/Em   Am     D      G
Middle Section
C      C      G      G
A      A      D      D
```

LET'S TWIST AGAIN
```
G      G      Em     Em
Am     Am     D      D
G      G      Em     Em
Am     D      G/C    G
C      C      G      G
C      C      D      D
G      G      Em     Em
Am     D      G/C    G/C
```

HANG ON SLOOPY
```
G/C    D      G      D/C
G      D      G      D/C
Chorus
G      D      G      D
G      D      G      D
```

SWEETS FOR MY SWEET
```
G/C    D/C    G/C    D/C
G/C    D/C    G/C    D/C
```

TRANSPOSING FROM THE KEY OF C MAJOR TO G MAJOR

The pitch level of songs was mentioned on page 12. If you had problems with singing melodies in the key of **C** major, you could change the music to the key of **G** major - in other words 'transpose' from **C** to **G**. When transposing from **C** to **G**, the melody notes will change in this way:

```
Key of C:  c    d    e    f    g    a    b
           ↓    ↓    ↓    ↓    ↓    ↓    ↓
Key of G:  g    a    b    c    d    e    f#
```

The chords will change in a similar way:

```
Key of C:  C    Dm   Em   F    G    Am
           ↓    ↓    ↓    ↓    ↓    ↓
Key of G:  G    Am   Bm   C    D    Em
```

As mentioned on page 18, there is a connection between key, chords and melody. When transposing music from one key to another, the relationship of the melody notes and chords remains the same. Playing songs in the key of **G** instead of **C** will sound the same except for the overall pitch level. The **g** note is the new fundamental or key note, and the **f** note has to be changed to **f#** in order to keep the note relationships the same. Scales and note relationships will be looked at again in Book 2.

A NOTE FROM THE AUTHOR

Congratulations on completing the first book of the course! You can now combine your right and left hands to produce a variety of rhythm patterns in two keys. This means you can handle a whole range of songs on your piano or keyboard already - try to use the styles you've learnt for songs you like that aren't too complicated to play.

Until you acquire the ability to work out songs from records (which will take a little time), you should look for the written music for songs either in separate sheet music or in songbooks - you'll see that the underlying chords are always given. You need to experiment with the styles and patterns you know to see which fits the particular song best.

In Book 2 you'll be taking your left and right hand co-ordination a stage further with more complicated but interesting rhythm patterns, more and different chords, bass runs and the swing style. To keep the notation simple, as well as to make your learning easier, the material in Book 2 (like that in this book) is written so only one hand actually presses down on the keys at one time. A variety of popular songs are used to illustrate the new techniques and styles as they were in Book 1.

Enjoy your playing *and* learning,

Printed in England
Panda Press · Haverhill · Suffolk • 10/92